Walking

30+ Walks Around Po

by

AJ Noon

Illustrations by KS Lawrence

Dedicated to Joe Noon, a man who rambled through history.

"From thence we went to Portsmouth town, and there viewed not only the town itself, and the haven, but also divers bulwarks ... In viewing of which we find the bulwarks chargeable, massy, well-rampaired; but ill-fashioned, ill-flanked, and set in unmeet places, the town weak in comparison of that it ought to be, too huge great (for within the walls are fair and large closes, and much vacant room), the haven notable great, and standing by nature easy to be fortified. And for the more strength thereof we have devised two strong castles on either side of the haven, at the mouth thereof... "

Edward VI, 1522

Publishing Information

1st Published September 2022

Version 1.41f_p

ISBN: 978-1-8384332-3-9

REDVARK PRODUCTIONS

www.redvarkpublishing.co.uk

redvarkpub@gmail.com

@redvarkpub

A ridiculous amount of thanks (as always) to KSL for her hard work

Map data copyrighted OpenStreetMap contributors and available from https://www.openstreetmap.org

Printed by Bishops Printers, Portsmouth, England

Postcards and prints scanned from the author's own collection

Contents

Fareham
Southwick
Havant
West Bo
Emsworth
Portsea
I. Thorney
Ile Hayling
PORTSMOUTH
GOSPORT
Southsea
Hayling
SPITHEAD
Ryde
Ile de Wight

Introduction

Portsea Island, the island on which Portsmouth and its numerous component communities exist, has been inhabited since the Bronze Age. It is a true island and is the third most densely populated city in the United Kingdom (after London and Luton, as of the 2021 census). The safe anchorages, firstly of Portsmouth Harbour and then off Spithead, led to the permanent presence of the Royal Navy and drove the expansion and development of the city you see now. Though there has been much rebuilding over the centuries, with some careful explorations there are plenty of fragments of history that still shine through, including Roman, Norman, Georgian, and World War II features.

The walks in this book are designed to give you a flavour of the key factors that have influenced Portsmouth, as well as helping to get you out and about. It would be impossible to tell all the history in one book, but I hope I provide enough snippets and pointers to allow you to get a real flavour for the areas you walk through, and to inspire you to investigate their history further.

Many of these walks are based on Portsea, but I have included areas beyond the island which have played key roles in the overall development of Portsmouth. There are only a few walks in Gosport which does not do justice to its own complex history, but they should help you to understand how the two sides of the harbour relied on and shaped each other (*right, looking out of the harbour towards the Solent, showing how narrow the entrance to the harbour is*).

Most of the walks are circular, and I have tried to ensure there are train stations, bus-stops, and/or parking close to each. You do not have to begin or end at a certain point, and many of the walks cross each other, so if the wind is fair and your legs are strong, there is nothing to stop you strolling into another section of history.

The best Ordnance Survey maps for these walks are OL3 for Portsmouth and west of Portsea Island, and OL8 for the east of Portsea Island, including Hayling and Thorney Islands. Alternatively, you can get custom maps printed from the Ordnance Survey, and if you choose 1:25000 scale and centre it on PO1 1AA it will cover all but a couple of these walks.

I have included altitude maps for walks that have anything more than 200 feet of climb to give you an indication of their profile. Portsmouth is very flat, so there are few walks in this book with much of a climb to test your stamina.

If you have suggestions, or corrections, then please get in touch.

AJ Noon

Symbology

The history icon indicates that the walk contains a high degree of historical features, such as buildings and fortifications.

You may be wondering why Hampshire has a rose as its emblem... Well so are many others. There is no clear explanation as to why, look at this blog post for some possible explanations: *https://britishcountyflags.com/2016/11/11/hampshireflag*

The nature icon alerts you to good chances for spotting wildlife.

If you see the museum icon then the walk passes by, or includes, a museum.

If you have a dog, then this is the icon to look for as the walk is suitable for your canine companion (I have not marked any of the city walks with the icon)

If you see the wheelchair icon, then the walk is suitable for wheelchairs (though some walks may have slight deviations to cater for them) and buggies.

The muddy or very muddy icons mean the walk can get muddy in winter or particularly damp weather.

Some sections can be flooded at high tide, so watch out!

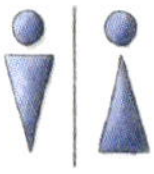

Public toilets are available on the route.

Pubs! If you need refreshment look for this sign.

If you see the picnic tables icon, then the walk passes by picnic tables available for public use.

The picnic blanket icon indicates there are grassy areas suitable for laying out a picnic blanket.

If you like frisbees or kite-flying, this is a walk for you.

If you see the geocaching icon, then there are one or more geocaches to find on the trail.

The compass indicates North, to help you align the maps correctly.

If you have not geocached before, it is an easy and fun activity to do while walking. You'll need to download the app (*right*) for your smartphone (there is a free option, and a paid subscription if you decide you want more features). Then, whilst on your walk, there are hidden '*treasure*' caches you need to find. Each cache should contain a trinket and a logbook. You sign the logbook and, if you decide to take the trinket, you replace it with something of equal value.

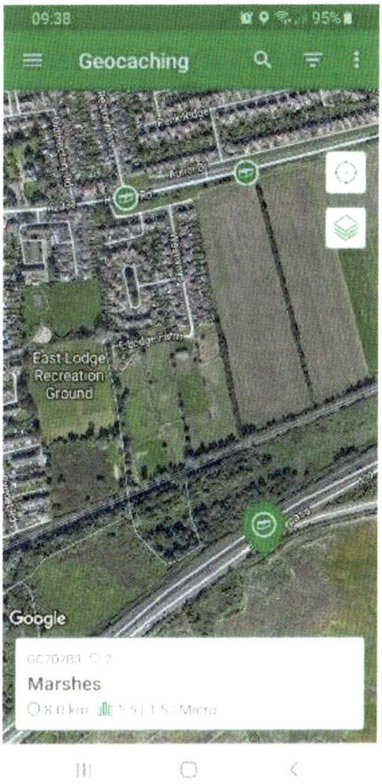

This is a great activity to keep kids entertained on a walk, and if you regularly walk in an area with no geocaches, you can create your own, upload it to the database, and then see who visits.

A B C D E F Letters in circles highlight key points in the walks, whether they be great observation points or obstacles to watch out for on the path and correlate the map with the text.

If you come across a public path that is blocked, damaged, overgrown, or has been fly-tipped, you can report issues here:
https://www.hants.gov.uk/landplanningandenvironment/rightsofway/reportaproblem

Victoria Barracks in 1909. Only one block remains of the barracks, which is now part of Portsmouth City Museum on Museum Road

If you spend any time on the internet, sooner or later you will come across a debate on '*what is Portsmouth*'? You certainly can't use the first part of the postcode, '*PO'*, as PO22 goes as far east as Bognor Regis and PO15 covers Whitely in the west. Some say it should only be PO1 to PO5, excluding PO6 which starts on the north bank of Portsea Creek, as everything in that postcode is '*off*' the island; including Paulsgrove, Cosham, and Drayton. Portsmouth City Council covers PO1 to PO6 which is the definition I am happy with - especially as I was born in Drayton. It is interesting to note that Nelson's Monument, on Portsdown Hill by Fort Nelson and surely claimed by Portsmouth, actually falls under Winchester Council.

Portsmouth is the United Kingdom's only island city, and Portsea Island covers 9.5 square miles, with its highest point - where Kingston Crescent meets Kingston Road - a whopping 21 feet above sea level! There are expected to be over 216,000 people living here by the end of 2022, with some 26,000 students enrolled at Portsmouth University (though not all live here). The name Portsea comes from the Latin: '*portus'* for harbour and the Saxon '*ea*', meaning island, so 'Portsea Island' is really a tautological '*Harbour Island Island*'.

In 1904, a Bronze Age hoard was discovered in Milton, and in 2003 a Saxon log boat was excavated from Langstone Harbour, so we know the island has had populations on or nearby for thousands of years, but hard evidence of settlements on Portsea is difficult to come by until the Domesday Book of 1086. It is believed Vikings raided the area in 787, but we do not know if they landed on Portsea or in the area of Portchester Castle, which was built in the late 3rd Century and is generally thought to have been the focus for the population in the area until the 12th Century.

It was the granting of a Royal Charter by King Richard I in 1194, and the creation of a '*Royal*' Dockyard by King John in 1212 that really cemented the future of Portsmouth and her key role in the defence of the nation.

Over the centuries, the large amounts of marshland and farmland that separated the communities such as Portsea, Kingston, Fratton, and Hilsea were reclaimed and built-on, leading to the conurbation we know now. If you look at this map from 1791 (*right*), you can see just how widely spread the communities were even as late as then. The area near Southsea Common was called the Little Morass, and the Canoe Lake area was known as the Great Morass. The Little Morass was drained from 1820, and the Great Morass was drained from 1886, both to allow development of the areas.

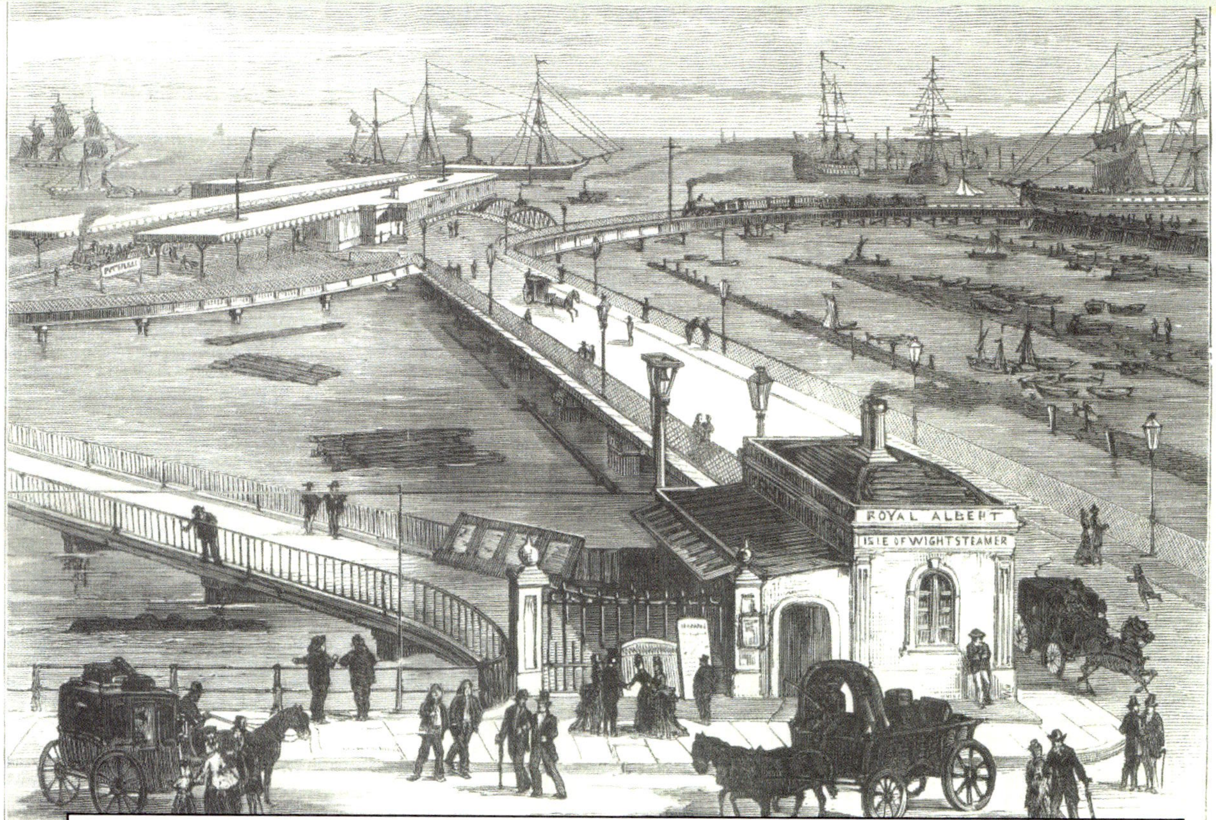

A View of The Hard, 1903, showing the railway spur leading into the dockyard

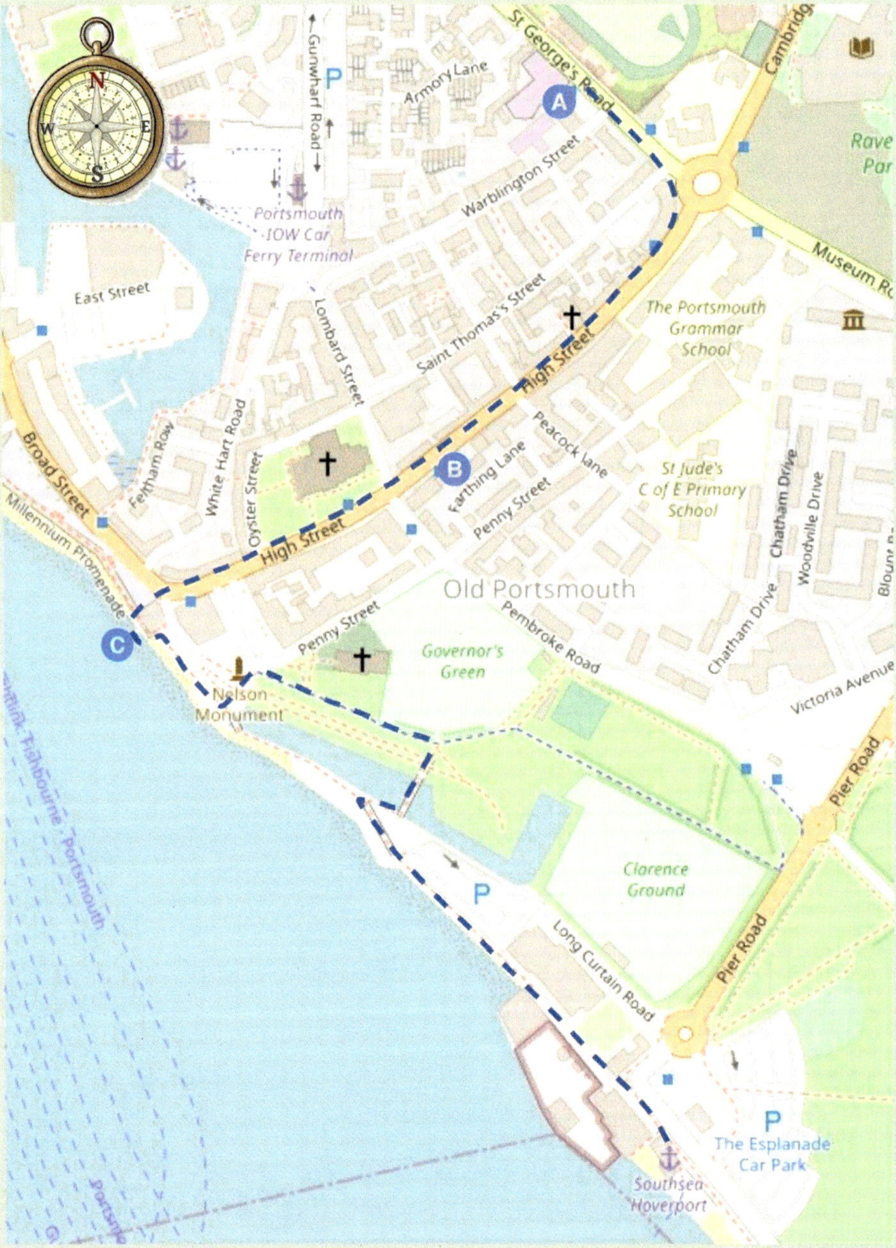
N
E
S
W
A
B
C
St George's Road
Cambridge
Museum Rd
Armory Lane
Gunwharf Road
P
Warblington Street
Portsmouth
IOW Car
Ferry Terminal
East Street
Lombard Street
Saint Thomas's Street
High Street
The Portsmouth
Grammar
School
Broad Street
Feltham Row
White Hart Road
Oyster Street
Peacock lane
Farthing Lane
Penny Street
St Jude's
C of E Primary
School
Chatham Drive
Woodville Drive
Millennium Promenade
Old Portsmouth
Pembroke Road
Penny Street
Governor's
Green
Victoria Avenue
Nelson
Monument
Pier Road
Clarence
Ground
Long Curtain Road
The Esplanade
Car Park
Southsea
Hoverport

P1. The Nelson Trail

1.15 Miles | 30 Mins | 15 Ft Ascent

All pavement

Parking: Garrison Church (Pay, Short Stay), PO1 2NJ, Clarence Pier Car Park (Pay), PO5 3XX

Bus: Cambridge Junction, 3, 23, 25, 700, Hoverbus

Nearest Train Station: Portsmouth and Southsea (.75 Miles)

Okay, so this isn't a 'proper' walk to start you off, but if you have any interest in the history of Portsmouth or the Royal Navy then re-tracing the footsteps of Vice-Admiral Horatio Nelson (*right*) when he left England for the fateful Battle of Trafalgar is a must.

A There are information boards along this walk at key places, and it starts at the Landport Gate, where St George's Road meets Warblington Street (PO1 2EJ). In pre-Norman times, Portchester was the main centre of activity in the area, with smaller settlements in the areas of Copnor, Fratton, Buckland, and Cosham, but in 1181 John of Gisors granted land centred around where Portsmouth Cathedral is now to the Augustinian monks. In 1189 Richard I (returning from captivity during the Crusades) granted Portsmouth a Royal Charter and ordered a dock to be built, half-a-mile north-west of where you are now standing (roughly where St George's Church is, outside of Gunwharf Quays).

As this area developed, it became clear that Portsmouth, the new docks, and the navy ships needed protecting, especially after the French sacked Portsmouth in 1338 during the Hundred Years' War. This led to fortifications being built around what is now called Old Portsmouth, and the Landport gate in front of you gets its name as it was the gate in the defences between the protected port area and the open land beyond. If you could step through the gate, then you would have been walking out of the old town.

By 1773, the area you are standing in was protected all the way to the sea (*left*), and a secondary enclosure protected the dockyard. It is important to note that the defences protected against attacks from seaward *and* landward in case an enemy force landed along the coast and tried to attack from behind (which was also the thinking behind the later Palmerston defences).

On the morning of September 14th, 1805, Horatio Nelson entered Portsmouth through this gate before readying to re-join *HMS Victory*, which was anchored out in the Solent. Nelson's carriage would have taken him to your right, heading east along St Georges Road. Follow the road until you reach the roundabout. *If you haven't visited Portsmouth City Museum before and want to, then continue straight on at this roundabout and is it a short distance ahead on your right (entry is free, but they do not open on Mondays).*

Turn right down High Street, which has witnessed some of the critical moments in the history of Portsmouth, keeping a sharp eye out for the blue plaques. Portsmouth Grammar School on your left is based on the site of the old Cambridge barracks (built in 1856), then comes *Ye Spotted Dogge*, which dates to 1523 and is where the Duke of Buckingham (who was very unpopular at the time) was assassinated in 1628. It gained such infamy that in 1661 Samuel Pepys visited specifically to see the room where the duke was killed.

Number 12, a few doors along, is where the papers were signed to form Portsmouth Football Club (PFC) in 1898. Football in Portsmouth has several interesting snippets; including Arthur Conan-Doyle playing in goal for them when they were an amateur team, the first floodlit League game being played at Fratton Park in 1956, and PFC holding the FA Cup for the longest continuous period of seven years - however, if you remember your history something more important happened in 1939 than Pompey winning the cup, and league and cup football was suspended until after the liberation of Europe!

B Continue along the High Street until you reach the houses set back from the road on your left hand-side, with two old gaslights in front. These are built on the site of the George Inn, which was destroyed during a bombing raid in World War II. It was here that Nelson ate breakfast, his last meal in England before heading to board his flagship.

By 1805, Nelson was already famous, and hugely popular, and crowds gathered outside the inn to catch a glimpse of him. To get to the *Victory* unnoticed, Nelson snuck out via the backdoor of the inn, and he would have crossed behind these houses towards the Garrison Church - for practical reasons we will take a detour and re-join his steps shortly.

Stay on the High Street, passing the cathedral on your right, until you reach the Square Tower, which was built in 1494. It has served several purposes, including the governor's residence, a meat store, and as a base for a semaphore (signalling) tower. Now it holds arts and crafts events, performance nights, and weddings. If you look closely at the tower as you approach, there is a gold bust of Charles I set into it, marking the return to England in 1623 of the then Prince Charles after failing to organise a marriage with the sister of the King of Spain.

To the right of the tower is a statue of a knot (*left*) which marks the *'First Fleet'* of 1787, the first European settlers who sailed from Portsmouth to Australia. There are also monuments along the wall to those who lost their lives in the Falkland's in 1982, and the settlers who left for Roanoke Island, America, in 1587 (the place often mentioned in treasure hunting programmes).

Go through the archway by the side of the tower and onto the walkway, getting your first proper sight of the Solent and the Isle of Wight ahead of you. Turn to your left (east), head up the stairs, and onto the wide fortified area, which is the old saluting platform, rebuilt to its current layout in 1568 (*see picture on Page 21*).

C At the end of the platform (still heading east towards the funfair), go down the stairs to the Nelson statue on your left. On your right is the Royal Garrison Church, originally known as the Domus Dei (*below, early 1900's*). This building, though it looks ruined, is run by English Heritage and is well worth a visit (normally open Tues to Sat from April to September). The church was built in 1212 but was severely damaged during World War II - so much so that the roof of the nave was never replaced. The chancel however, tucked away inside, is stunning and should not be missed, despite outward appearances.

Walk down the path between the church and the ramparts until you come to a tunnel heading under the fortifications. It is believed Nelson walked through here and down to the beach, where a boat took him out to Spithead (*see map on Page 4*) and the awaiting *HMS Victory*. The public caught up with him here and cheered him out to sea, expecting him to soon engage the French and Spanish fleet assembled by Napoleon.

Head through the tunnel and across the bridge, then once you have admired the view turn to the funfair on your left and head through it. On the other side, by the hovercraft terminal, is a plinth topped by an anchor from *HMS Victory*, commemorating the Battle of Trafalgar on 21st October, 1805, where Nelson lost his life.

This is the end of the Nelson trail, and the short introduction to Old Portsmouth. Now would be a good time to grab an ice-cream and watch the hovercraft come and go. If you have the time, and the weather is nice, carry on to Southsea Castle, and then follow the Millennium Promenade (***Walk P2***) back to the dockyard.

Queen Street
South Camber
A
Havant Street
College Street
Portsea
University of Portsmouth - North Zone
Victoria Park
A3
Station Street
Portsmouth and Southsea
Greetham Street
Portsmouth Harbour
West Coastway Line
Park Road
United Services Rugby Ground
Hyde Park Road
Gunwharf Quays
HMS Temeraire
Burnaby Road
Winston Churchill Avenue
B
St George's Road
Cambridge Road
A288
Melbourne Place
Middle Street
St James's Road
Grosvenor Street
Wightlink Car Ferry Terminal
Ravelin Park
St Pauls Road
King Street
Yorke Street
C
Saint Thomas's Street
High Street
B2154
Kings Road
Elm Grove
Broad Street
White Hart Road
Penny Street
Woodville Drive
Flint Street
Stone Street
Castle Road
D
Old Portsmouth
Pembroke Road
Victoria Avenue
St Edward's Road
Garden Lane
Southsea
Queens Crescent
Kent Road
Pier Road
Duisburg Way
A288
P
Southsea Common
Osborne Road
Southsea Hoverport
Clarence Parade
Stanley Street
Clarendon Road
Clarence Esplanade
Avenue De Caen
P
E
N
W
E
S

P2. The Millennium Promenade

2.5/3 Miles **1 Hour** **32 Ft Ascent**

All pavement

Parking: Gunwharf Quays (Pay), PO1 3TZ, Historic Dockyard (Pay), PO1 3LJ

Bus: The Hard (lots of routes terminate here)

Nearest Train Station: Portsmouth Harbour (.15 Miles)

The second walk everyone should do is the Millennium Promenade, another short walk that is non-circular but takes you past some of the key elements that made Portsmouth crucial to the Royal Navy.

You can walk this route in either direction, but I prefer to start from the gates of the Historic Dockyard, follow it through to Portsmouth Point, and then along the seafront to finish at Southsea Castle. Alternatively, if you have just walked the Nelson Trail (**Walk P1**) then you can follow this route back to the dockyard.

Under normal circumstances (e.g., not a pandemic or a security alert) it is possible to walk around the dockyard site for free between 12 and 4, though you won't be able to go onto the ships or into the galleries. Go to the Visitor Centre and ask for the free 'Historic Quarter Pass', then walk down to the far end, around the outside of HMS Victory, then head back to the main gates, making the overall walk length 3 miles. If you are lucky, you may see one of the new aircraft carriers or the Type 45 destroyers tied up near HMS Victory. NB dogs are not allowed in the Historic Dockyard.

A Starting at the dockyard gates, about twenty feet in front of them is a bollard set into the pavement, with an anchor chain motif engraved into the stones leading from it (*left*). This chain motif is the path to follow (there are a couple of breaks in the chain, but it is easy enough to keep track of).

This area, the Hard, has always been a landing area for small boats and was constructed in its current layout in 1720. The term *'Hard'* comes from the fact there used to be hard clay here rather than mud, providing a solid area to launch and recover boats from. Head along the Hard, keeping the harbour on your right, and if you look closely at the bollards in this area you will see they resemble the forward half of a naval gun. Some of the ones closer to the bus station, and the ones embedded against the dockyard gate walls, are actual guns. When the weapons were no longer needed, they were often buried halfway to be used as bollards, and the design for the modern bollards you see were based on these.

Follow the chain motif as it takes you past the bus and train stations, and then through the underpass on your right. The area you are now entering, Gunwharf Quays, was built as a shopping and entertainment centre which opened in 2001, but prior to that it had served as part of the Royal Navy base for nearly three hundred years. It was here that the navy tested and stored their ordnance, hence the name *'gun wharf'*.

B Carry on past the shops until you come to the pontoons with the small boats moored. On your right is the Spinnaker Tower; opened in 2005 (only 5 years later than planned), and 560 feet high, it is one of the tallest structures outside London that you can climb. There is an observation level with a glass floor towards the top of the 'sail'.

The route now leads to your left and, keeping the harbour mouth on your right, follow the chain past the shops and restaurants, then past the new flats until you reach the Isle of Wight ferry terminal. Take care crossing here as it gets busy with cars entering/exiting the ferry. The trail takes you past some public toilets, then bends to the right where you can see a small port for the local fishing fleet, called *'the Camber'*. The Camber is the oldest harbour in Portsmouth and was the heart of the trade and fishing fleets until ships grew too large for these docks. In 1586, the English explorer Sir Ralph Lane returned from the doomed Roanoke settlement with the assistance of Sir Francis Drake, bringing tobacco and potatoes to sell.

Benches: Plenty along the seafront

Picnic Areas: Best area by Southsea Castle

Pubs (Many): Too many to list, mainly at the start of the walk though

Public Toilets: Gunwharf, the Camber, the Round Tower

Cafes: Several

Shops: Gunwharf

The large modern building across from you, with the Union flag engraved into the main door, was the headquarters for Sir Ben Ainslie's America's Cup yacht racing team but is now outsourced as office and workshop spaces.

C Keep following the chain as it winds to the right through Portsmouth Point, also known as Spice Island, then back round to the left where you come to the Still and West pub, which has long been a family favourite for stopping off for a drink to watch the ships sail by (if you do go in don't forget to look up at the ceiling). The nickname Spice Island was earned for the *'spice of life'* that could be found here, whether it be exotic cargo and animals newly arrived, or the things such as fresh food and women that sailors had missed on their long journeys at sea.

Carry on to the open section of the fortifications looking out across the harbour mouth. There are records of great chains being commissioned to cross this stretch of water to protect the harbour. If an enemy fleet was incoming, the chain would be raised from the seabed and pulled taut across the harbour, preventing access. There is a sample of one of the chains on the ground behind you here, and we know of chains from 1522, 1664, and 1801. The building to your right is Tower House (*above, with the Round Tower*) and is where the artist William Wyllie lived between 1906 and 1931. He was buried in the grounds of Portchester Castle with honours for his work in saving naval history, including *HMS Victory*.

D The main tower - aptly named the Round Tower - was first constructed in wood in 1418, rebuilt in stone in 1490, and defends the harbour entrance. Take the stairs through the defences and along the walls to the Square Tower (see Page 13 for details of this tower). There are several art shops and a café built into the defences underneath you if you want to browse or stop for refreshments. Carry on along the old saluting platform (*Page 21, in 1842*) and follow the seafront all the way to Southsea Castle (when you reach the aquarium keep to the right-hand path by the sea). **For wheelchair users, just head along the hotwalls and past the Square Tower until you come out by the statue of Nelson.**

The castle itself, built in 1544 on the orders of Henry VIII, is free to visit and there is also a café inside the walls. Before you go inside, find the viewing scope in front of the castle looking out at the Isle of Wight. There are three green-topped channel warning markers in the sea just in front of it. Look out into the Solent, and ahead of you to the right is Spitbank Fort (*see Page 133*), constructed by 1878, and to the left three large yellow channel markers, put in to help direct the Royal E Navy's newest aircraft carriers.

Now, walk round to the front of the castle and enter, though to get onto the castle ramparts there are several sets of stairs, so it is not ideal for anyone with mobility issues.

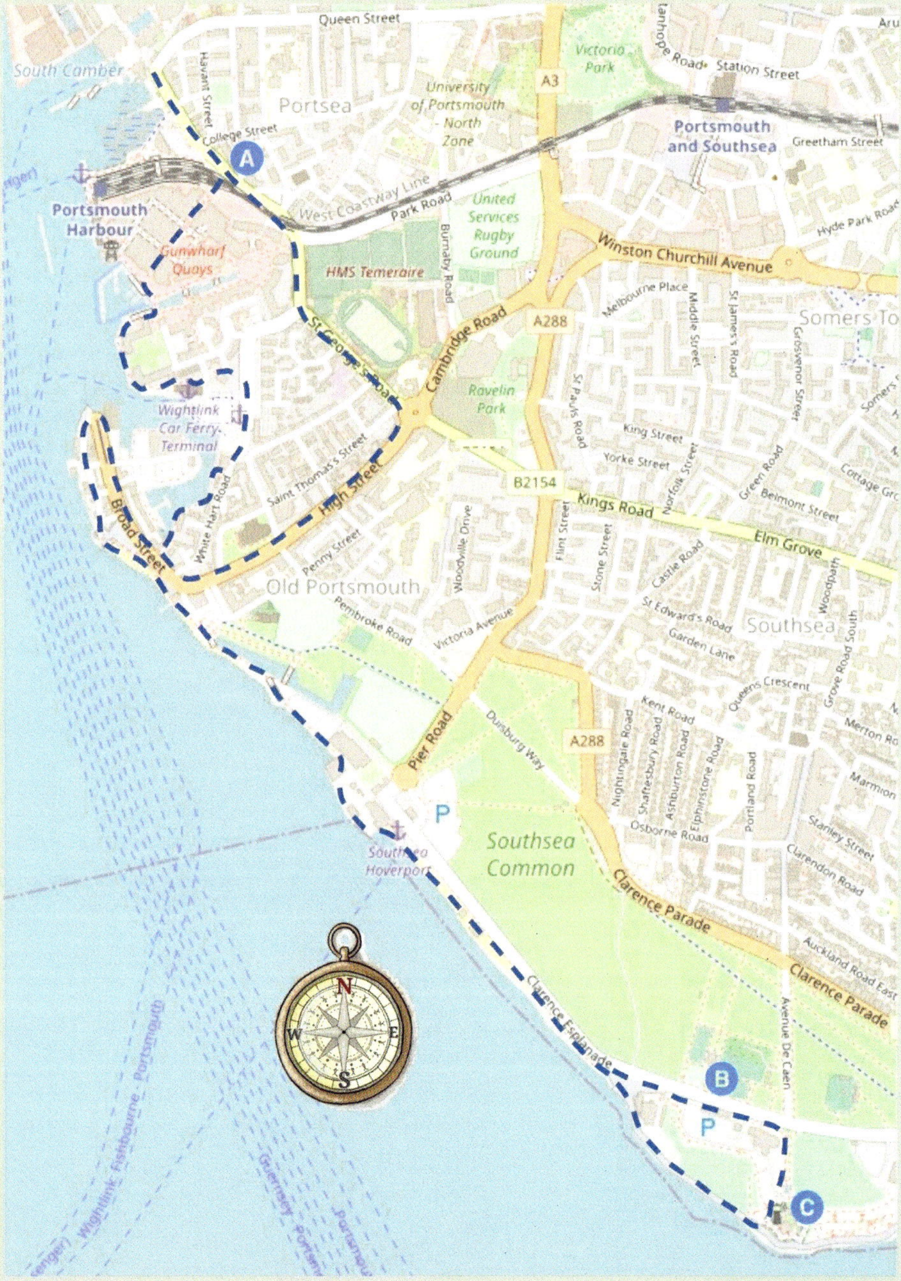
Queen Street
South Camber
Portsea
University of Portsmouth - North Zone
Victoria Park
A3
Station Street
Portsmouth and Southsea
Greetham Street
Hyde Park Road
Havant Street
College Street
A
Portsmouth Harbour
West Coastway Line
Park Road
Burnaby Road
United Services Rugby Ground
Winston Churchill Avenue
Gunwharf Quays
HMS Temeraire
Cambridge Road
A288
Melbourne Place
Middle Street
St James's Road
Grosvenor Street
Somers Town
St George's Road
Ravelin Park
Wightlink Car Ferry Terminal
St Paul's Road
King Street
Yorke Street
Norfolk Street
Green Road
Belmont Street
Cottage Grove
Saint Thomas's Street
High Street
B2154
Kings Road
Elm Grove
Broad Street
White Hart Road
Penny Street
Woodville Drive
Flint Street
Stone Street
Castle Road
Woodpath
Old Portsmouth
Pembroke Road
Victoria Avenue
St Edward's Road
Garden Lane
Southsea
Queens Crescent
Grove Road South
Kent Road
Merton Road
Pier Road
Duisburg Way
A288
Nightingale Road
Shaftesbury Road
Ashburton Road
Elphinstone Road
Portland Road
Marmion Road
Osborne Road
Stanley Street
P
Southsea Hoverport
Southsea Common
Clarendon Road
Clarence Parade
Auckland Road East
Clarence Parade
Clarence Esplanade
Avenue De Caen
B
P
C
N
W
E
S
Wightlink: Fishbourne - Portsmouth

P3. (P1+P2) Old Portsmouth Loop

5 Miles | 2 Hours | 50 Ft Ascent

All pavement

Parking: Gunwharf Quays (Pay), PO1 3TZ, Historic Dockyard (Pay), PO1 3LJ

Bus: The Hard (lots of routes terminate here)

Nearest Train Station: Portsmouth Harbour

Neither walks **P1** or **P2** are particularly long but are important for the history they cover. By combining them you can get a far more satisfying (and circular) walk. Starting from the dockyard gates, walk along the Hard towards the entrance to Gunwharf Quays (just past the train station), but instead of taking the underpass to your right, keep straight on until you come to a tree-lined square on your left.

A In the centre of this is a memorial to Isambard Kingdom Brunel (*left*), who was born on a street here that was destroyed in the heavy bombing Portsmouth suffered during World War II. His father, Marc Isambard Brunel, created the first ever mass production line at the dockyard at Portsmouth. Blocks, used in the rigging for the ships, used to be created by hand, but Marc Brunel linked three rows of his new machines to change this from a hand-crafted art to a machined process. By 1808 the block mills were producing over 130,000 blocks per year, but it also put hundreds of skilled craftsmen out of work.

Carry straight on, crossing Park Road (the entrance to the car park for Gunwharf Quays), and follow St. George's Road as it turns left. Half-way down this road, on your left you come to the Landport Gate, which is the starting point for **Walk P1**, the Nelson Trail. Follow the Nelson Trail as described, then once you have reached the anchor by the hoverport, continue to Southsea Castle.

Clarence Pier, which you have just passed, was the site of '*The Battle of Southsea*' in 1874. The city decided to close the public footpath between the pier and Old Portsmouth. This led to four days of rioting as people protested the loss of their freedom to walk, and it resulted in the Riot Act being read. The protestors won though, which is why the common remains undeveloped and free to roam.

When you get to a fork in the promenade at the aquarium, keep by the road rather than the seafront and it will take you past the D-Day Story.

B Outside the D-Day Story is LCT 7074 (*above*), which is the only surviving British Landing Craft Tank from D-Day. On the day, she carried 10 tanks and their crews over to Normandy, yet after World War II she ended up as a floating nightclub in Liverpool!

The D-Day Story also houses the Overlord Embroidery, which comprises 34 panels totalling 272 feet in length (42 feet longer than the surviving sections of the Bayeux Tapestry). The Overlord Embroidery was finished in 1974 and tells the story of D-Day, it even incorporates material from the soldiers' uniforms. The museum opened in 1984 but underwent an extensive renovation and re-branding in 2018.

C Walk round to Southsea Castle (*left*), and you can do **Walk P2**, the Millennium Promenade, in reverse to take you back to the dockyard.

View from the Saluting Platform, 1842

St Helens Parade
Craneswater Park
Craneswater Avenue
Albert Road
Highland Road
Highland Cemetery
Eastern Parade
Esplanade
Mini Golf
Eastney Beach
St George's Road
Cromwell Road
Eastney Road
Goldsmith Avenue
A2030
Milton Road
A288
Milton Park
Milton
Eastney
Bransbury Park
Bransbury Road
Locksway Road
Furze Lane
Longshore Way
Eastney Lake
University of Portsmouth - Langstone Campus
Fort Cumberland Road
Ferry Road
Lumsden Road
Fraser Range (Disused)
Sewage Works
Lock Lake
West Winner
A
B
C
D
E
N
S
W
E

P4. Canals, Lumps, and Beams

5/6 Miles | 2 Hours 15 Mins | 23 Ft Ascent

Pavement, Shingle, Possibility of Mud

Parking: Canoe Lake Car Park, PO4 9RU (Pay, £4.20 for 3 hours)

Bus: South Parade Pier D, 23, X28

Nearest Train Station: Fratton (1.5 Miles)

For this walk, the first thing you need to do is check the tide times – Google *'Portsmouth Tide Times'* - as you want to do this walk at low tide. There is an optional route if the tide is high, but it is much better to do this as a beach walk.

Starting from the car park at Canoe Lake (or any of the spaces along the promenade there), head east. You will pass Southsea Model Village and the Rose Gardens (occupying Lumps Fort, see Page 44). When you reach the Coffee Cup café on the beach, there are toilets opposite, and you should notice the remains of fortifications on your left, which was Eastney Battery West, finished in 1863 and equipped with 11 guns to provide coastal defences. Slightly further ahead, are the remains of Eastney Battery East, which was built to the same specifications. There is currently no public access to either of these remains.

A As you walk past the battery, you come to the grand buildings of what was the Royal Marines Barracks. These buildings were constructed in the 1860's, and in the late 1940's became the HQ for the Royal Marines Hampshire units until its closure in 1991. A museum for the Royal Marines was established on the site in 1958, which closed in 2017 (with a plan to be incorporated into Portsmouth Historic Dockyard), and the Officer's Mess is now being redeveloped as a five-star hotel. One of the most notable features is the *'Yomper'* statue (*left*). It was unveiled in 1992 to commemorate the role the Royal Marines played in the liberation of the Falklands in 1982.

During that conflict, Royal Marines (and Parachute Regiment servicemen) had to march across the islands after the loss of the *Atlantic Conveyor* and her helicopters. They covered 56 miles in 3 days whilst carrying 36kg of pack each and across difficult terrain, which is known as a *yomp*.

B A bit further along, you come to Eastney Swimming Baths, which was built for the Royal Marines in 1904. It is now closed and due to be replaced by a development at Bransbury Park further to the North. There are public toilets here, and instead of following the road you now want to carry on along the beach, towards the brick building in the distance (*below*). On your left are large square concrete blocks – these are remains of the anti-tank defences constructed in the Second World War to help prevent any invasion from the sea in this area.

C After the caravans, an alley leads down the side of the fencing around the brick building. Take this alley until you reach an open space, where you will need to step-over the low barriers then follow the grass path along the fence to the right.

The buildings you are passing are the remains of Fraser Range, which was the training and test centre for Royal Naval gunnery. Gunnery practice ceased there in the 1980's, with the site closing in 2006. There are plans to develop a 'sympathetic' residential estate here, though there has been no real movement on this for a while.

D Following the grass path, you come to Ferry Road, and you now have the option to do the 5-mile walk or the 6-mile walk. If you want to do 6, turn to your right and walk up to the Hayling Ferry and back, passing Southsea Marina (*below left*). There are some picnic benches by the lifeguard station there, as well as a mobile café selling drinks and snacks.

E Otherwise, turn left and then follow Ferry Road bending to the right until you reach the seashore. Take the path in the grass following the road, where at the end it drops down to the beach. If the tide is low enough, head onto the beach and continue round the headland (*above*) all the way until you get to the Thatched House pub (*bottom*). Just after the pub, the beach slopes up so you can join the car park, and on your right is a bridge across the old canal entrance. Cross this bridge, then head left down the alley which brings you out on Locksway Road.

The canal originally ran from Ford to Portsmouth, with our section opening in 1822 and running from the locks where you are now standing (*main picture*), through Milton and Fratton, and terminating near where Portsmouth and Southsea train station is now. Goldsmith Avenue from Milton Park to Fratton follows the route of the canal, and the railway from Fratton follows the rest of the route. Unfortunately, the canal used seawater, which contaminated the fresh-water wells on the island, and it closed in 1855.

Walk along Locksway Road, passing the remains of St. James Hospital on your right. It was opened as a sanatorium for infectious diseases in 1879 and transitioned to mental health care from 1914. The site has now mostly been sold for property re-development.

On your left, when the road starts to bend to the right, is a footpath between two buildings (close to a bus stop, with trees growing in the middle of the path). Take this path between the houses which goes straight to Milton Road (it is the old canal towpath, so is very straight). Follow Milton Road south to the roundabout and take Cromwell Road on the opposite side. Pass Bransbury Park on your left, where further down that road is the Eastney Beam Engine House, run by Portsmouth Museums. Opening times are generally the last Sunday of the month (www.eastneyenginehouses.co.uk) and are worth a visit if you can get there when they are open. The two huge pumps inside were built in 1887 and were used to pump sewage out to sea.

Follow Cromwell Road as it bends past the Eastney Barracks, then take Eastern Parade on your left, which takes you back to Canoe Lake and then the starting car park.

Benches: Along the seafront

Picnic Areas: Near the Hayling ferry

Pubs: The Thatched House, The Old Oyster House

Public Toilets: Canoe Lake, Eastney

Cafes: Multiple

Shops: Along Eastney Road

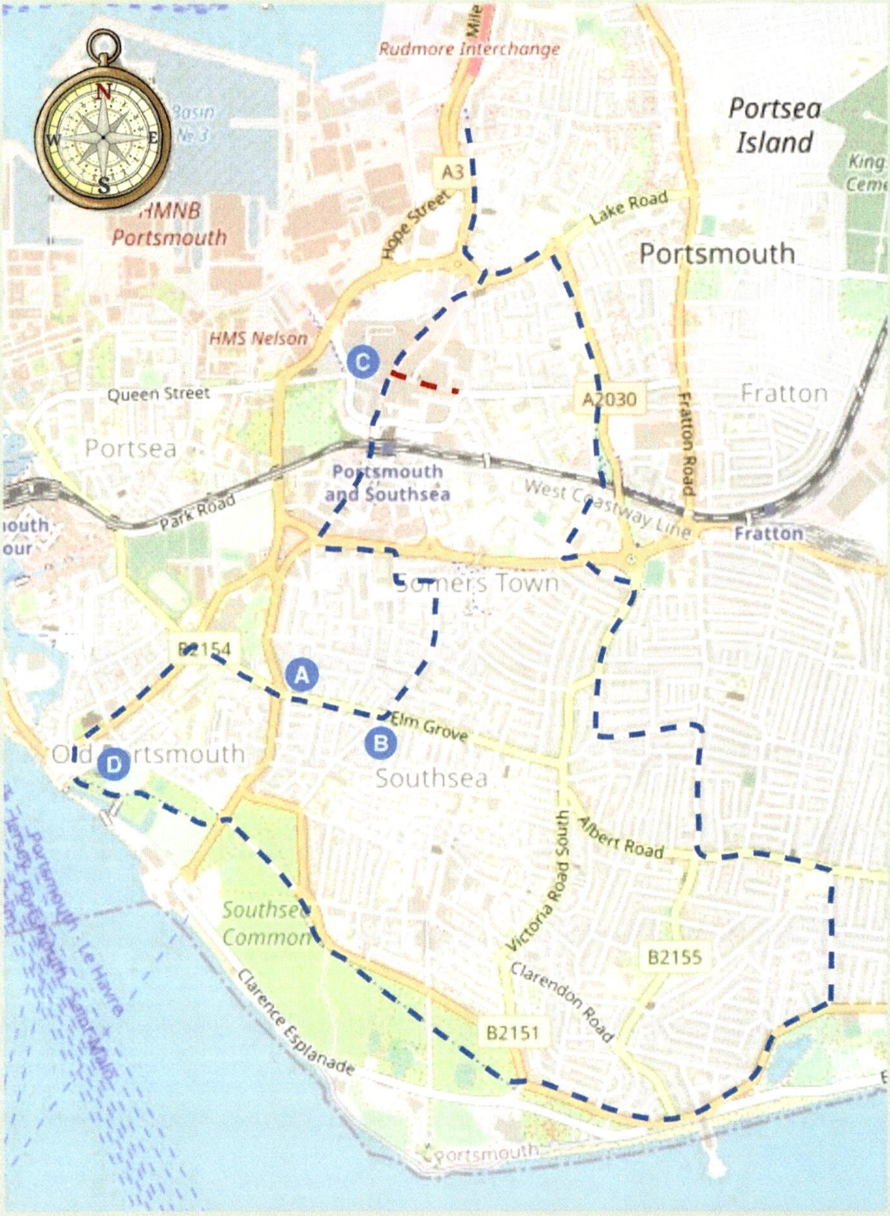
Rudmore Interchange
Portsea Island
Basin No 3
HMNB Portsmouth
A3
Hope Street
Lake Road
Portsmouth
HMS Nelson
C
A2030
Fratton
Queen Street
Fratton Road
Portsea
Portsmouth and Southsea
West Coastway Line
Park Road
Fratton
Somers Town
B2154
A
Elm Grove
B
Old Portsmouth
D
Southsea
Albert Road
Victoria Road South
Southsea Common
B2155
Clarendon Road
Clarence Esplanade
B2151

P5. Literary Portsmouth

6.25 Miles | 3 Hours | 10 Ft Ascent

All pavement

Parking: Garrison Church on the road (Pay, £4.60 for 4 Hours)

Bus: St Thomas Cathedral, 25

Nearest Train Station: Portsmouth and Southsea (on the route)

This walk introduces you to some of the literary figures who have, at one time or another, called Portsmouth home. There are a couple of museums on the route as well, so you may want to allocate more time (and parking money) if you plan on visiting these. Portsmouth Museum does not open on Mondays, and the very helpful Charles Dickens Birthplace Museum (www.charlesdickensbirthplace.co.uk) only opens on selected dates, so please check in advance. If you live in a PO1 to PO6 postcode, access is free with proof, otherwise it costs £4.50 for an adult. They also have a dedicated walk on Dickens you can download, called *'The Dickens Trail'*.

Portsmouth Cathedral (*right*), the starting point, is well worth a visit, and there is an audio tour available for your phone. From here, head north up the High Street (see page 12) to the roundabout. Turn right onto Museum Road, passing Portsmouth Museum and Art Gallery, which has a large collection on Sir Arthur Conan-Doyle inside (free to visit).

A At the next roundabout, go straight ahead onto Kings Road (which turns into Elm Grove). The first buildings on the left are where Hyde's Drapery Emporium once stood, and it was here that H.G. Wells started an apprenticeship. He hated his time there (reflected in his novel *The History of Mr. Polly*) and finally quit, walking back to Uppark House where his mother was a housekeeper.

B A bit further along on your right, after the more recent builds, is a plaque on the wall marking where Sir Arthur Conan-Doyle lived for 8 years. The original building is no longer standing, but the first two Sherlock Holmes Books were written here (*A Study in Scarlet, 1887,* and *The Sign of the Four, 1890*). He wrote these whilst running a medical practice and still found time to play in goal for Portsmouth Association Football Club, an amateur outfit that was disbanded two years before Portsmouth F.C. came into being.

On your left, by the garage, is Green Road. Head to the end of this (it turns into Grosvenor Street), then bear left onto Waterloo Street at the end, then turn right. This leads to Winston Churchill Avenue, where you cross to your left, and keep going until you reach Guildhall Walk (by the Astoria nightclub). The nightclub was originally The Palace Cinema, opening in 1921, and was designed by A.E. Cogswell, a name synonymous with Portsmouth architecture (see page 32). It closed as a cinema in 1981 and eventually became a nightclub.

Go along Guildhall Walk, passing the New Theatre Royal, which had several rebuilds (the last in 1900). They do very good behind-the-scenes tours there if you get the chance to go on one. You then reach the Guildhall itself (*above, circa 1934*) and its statue of Charles Dickens (*main picture*). The Guildhall was built in 1890, and used to stand proud and un-enclosed, though it was heavily damaged in the bombings of World War II, leading to it being rebuilt. Then, in the early 1970's the decision was passed to build the new civic offices and the library, and the Guildhall became surrounded by the glass and concrete structures you see now.

C Carry on past the train station and into Commercial Road. At the fountain keep ahead, though you can take a diversion to your right down Arundel Street and back to discover some of the literary etchings in the pavement there. There are public toilets in Cascades if you need them, then at the top end of Commercial Road bear right onto Lake Road, where there is an underpass on your left. Take the underpass and use the stairs on the left after going under the road. Follow the buildings round, passing All Saints Church, then cross at the pedestrian crossing. Ahead is an archway which leads to the Charles Dickens Birthplace Museum (*left*). You will also see a set of the few remaining tramlines left in Portsmouth (*opposite, bottom*). When you have visited, return to this point, then take a left onto Church Street as it passes behind the church. At the next roundabout go straight ahead down Holbrook Road, and cross the next roundabout (by Asda), staying on the right-hand side of the road. You pass a small playpark, then the path takes you over a railway bridge and onto Sommers Road.

When you reach the dual carriageway, turn left and on your right is Bradford Road running alongside the little ships and the mosque. The mosque was originally The Plaza cinema, opening in 1928, then was The Gaumont, then a bingo hall. At the mosque, turn right down Victoria Road North and stay on it until the bend in the road, where you go past the planters and onto Outram Road. This leads to Campbell Road, which you turn left into. Just ahead, on your right, is a blue plaque marking the house where Rudyard Kipling lived between 1871 and 1877.

At the end of Campbell Road, turn right onto Lawrence Road, then when you reach Albert Road head to your left, passing the Trinity Methodist Church (1901) and Craneswater Junior School (1910, A.E. Cogswell). When you reach the Festing Pub, head right down Festing Road, taking the second left, Salisbury Road, when you reach it. On your right is Helena Road, where there is a plaque for the author Nevil Shute, with the house next door having a blue plaque for Commander Edward Unwin, who received a Victoria Cross for his action at Gallipoli in 1915 (house #'s 12 and 14).

At the end of the road, you come back out to Eastern Parade with Canoe Lake to your right. Head to the seafront and follow it all the way back to the cathedral. You can take the promenade for a sea view or go through the paths on Southsea Common if you want a bit of green and trees.

D Finally, if you are after an antique, or a print or a postcard, then you would do well to pop into Sally Antiques in the old Sally Port Inn (*above right*). They have multiple floors to explore, and it also happens to be next door to a decent bar. The Sally Port Inn is where Lionel 'Buster' Crabbe was staying when he disappeared in 1956 whilst allegedly diving under a visiting Russian warship.

Benches: Along the seafront

Picnic Areas: Near the Hayling ferry

Pubs: The Thatched House, The Old Oyster House

Public Toilets: Canoe Lake, Eastney

Cafes: Multiple

Shops: Along Eastney Road

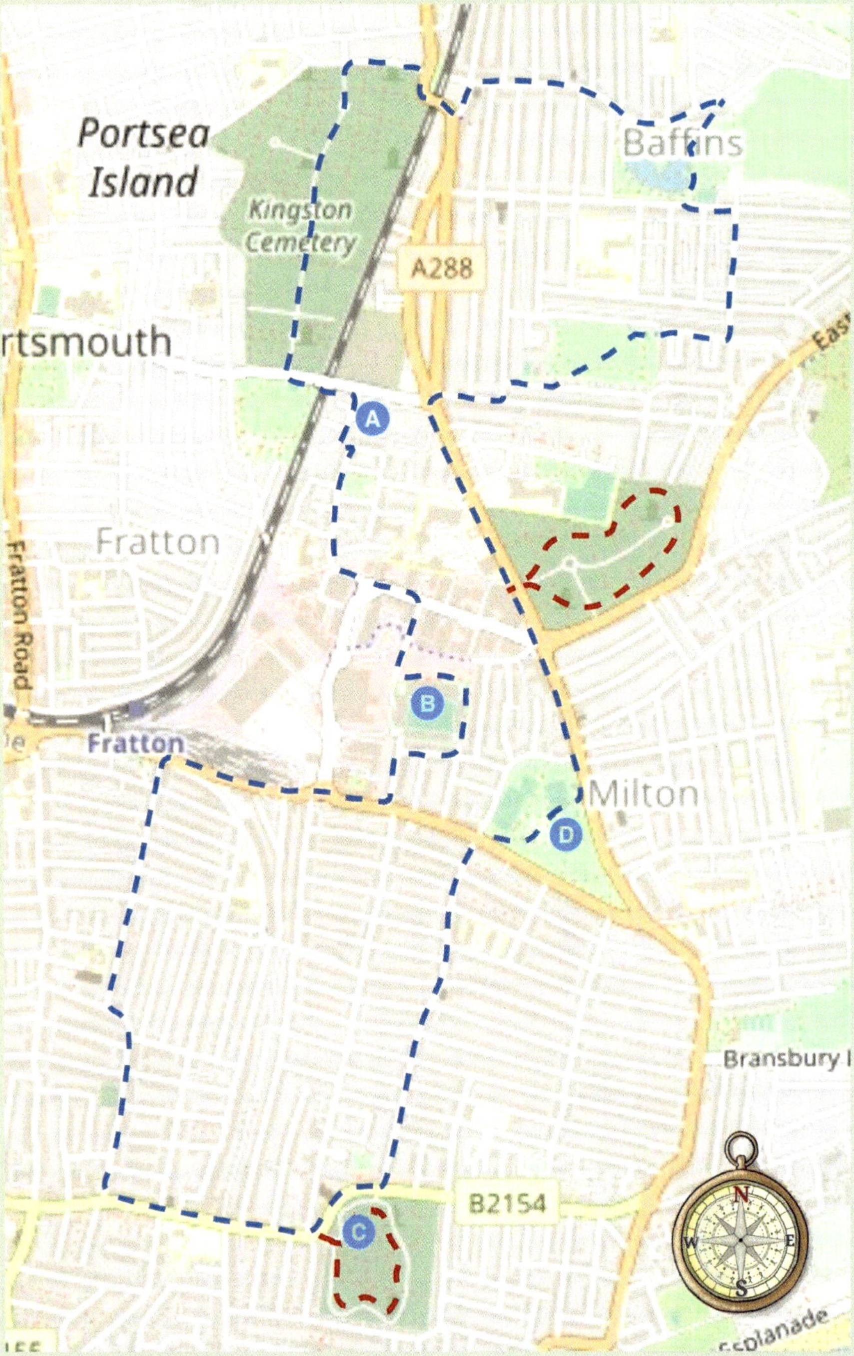
Portsea Island
Kingston Cemetery
A288
Baffins
rtsmouth
Fratton
Fratton Road
Fratton
Milton
Bransbury
B2154
Esplanade
A
B
C
D
N
S
E
W

P6. Parks and Remembrance

5.75 Miles | 2 Hours | 23 Ft Ascent

All pavement

Parking: Baffins Pond, PO3 6PG (Free, open dawn to dusk)

Bus: Westover Road, 14

Nearest Train Station: Fratton (.5 Miles)

There have been over a hundred different places of worship within the Portsmouth boundaries, and though some no longer remain (or are practising venues), they have all left an imprint on the landscape. The three large cemeteries of Kingston, Milton, and Highland Road are great places for contemplation and casual strolling and contain a wealth of wildlife. All three are open from 9am (often earlier) until 4 pm (later in summer).

From the free car park at Baffins Pond, walk along Tangier Road so you pass the pond on your left. At the end, by St. Joseph's Church, follow the road round to the left then cross over the railway bridge on your right. New Road on your left takes you to the entrance of Kingston Cemetery, and follow the main path down through the graveyard. This is Portsmouth's largest cemetery, covering some 52 acres, and opened in 1856. There is a stunning array of tombstones and statues throughout the grounds, and there are plenty of grey squirrels to keep you company as you walk.

Exiting onto St. Mary's Road (there should be a play park opposite you), head left over the railway bridge and then right down Whitcombe Gardens. You should have noticed the remains of Kingston Prison on your left, which is now a residential development. It opened in 1877 to host male B and C category offenders, but was closed in 2013, and Leslie Grantham, who appeared in *Eastenders* as *'Dirty Den'*, once served a stretch of time there.

A On Whitcombe Gardens, pass a small basketball court and next to it is an alley. Take the alley, turning right into Union Road which takes you down to Rodney Road and the relatively new units and developments. Head left along Rodney Road then take a right down Anson Road. At the end (by the Portsmouth F.C. shop) is an alley, Milton Lane, which takes you past Fratton Park. At the end of the lane, turn right down Speck Lane, so you are passing the *'away'* end of Fratton Park. The lane eventually meets Carisbrooke Road, where you turn right to take you to Frogmore Road and the entrance to Fratton Park (*left*).

B A.E. Cogswell moved to Portsmouth in the 1870's and started an apprenticeship with the architect George Rake. Cogswell went on to design pubs, banks, libraries, churches and cinemas across Portsmouth, and though many were lost in the blitz and later re-developments, you can find numerous examples of his work in the city. *The Pompey Pub*, to the left of the main Fratton Park entrance (*above*) was designed by him and he also designed the club's first south stand.

From Frogmore Road, walk down to Goldsmith Avenue and turn right, following it until you reach The Talbot pub (*right*). You can probably guess who designed this pub too... Head down Talbot Road, bearing left at the end where it turns into Fawcett Road, passing the Golden Eagle pub. On your right is the Jewish Cemetery (no public access) and then you reach the junction with the Bold Forrester and the Leopold pubs. Go left, following Highland Road until it reaches Highland Road Cemetery.

The side gates are rarely opened, so you have to enter here, explore, and then return to this point.

C This cemetery opened in 1854, and the *'Friends of Highland Road Cemetery'* have done a lot of work in making the history of the site readily available. Their updates are featured on a noticeboard just inside the gates. Also note the large cross you see first, (*left*), which is for members of the Brickwood family.

Brickwoods were one of big breweries in Portsmouth, having started in 1851 in Arundel Street, moving to the Portsmouth Brewery in 1902. They took on the name of Portsmouth Brewery in 1953, but you can still find traces of *'Brickwoods'* all over Portsea Island.

Tucked away in the south of the site you should find a large mausoleum to the Dupree family (*below*). They also have a brewing connection, having founded Portsmouth United Breweries, and were heavily active in politics and the development of the city.

When you have completed you exploration come back to the entrance and go right along Highland Road until you reach Winter Road. Follow this all the way to Goldsmith Avenue (the old canal route) and enter Milton Park.

D Head through the park to the opposite corner, and you will pass The Barn, the home of the acting troupe the Portsmouth Players (www.portsmouthplayers.co.uk). They perform here, and at other venues in the city, and have been performing since 1927.

The exit to the park brings you to Milton Road, head to your left and continue until you reach Milton Cemetery. This opened in 1912, in the week the Titanic sank, and one of the survivors, a member of the victualling crew Sidney Daniels, is buried here. It is also a great place to spot wildlife, especially foxes (*below*) early in the morning or in the evenings.

Leave the cemetery and continue up to the roundabout, taking Langstone Road on your right. The second left is Lichfield Road, and then Walsall Road on the right. Enter Tamworth Park, crossing to the opposite corner, then follow the path in the estate as it takes you to Marina Grove on your left. This leads to Hayling Avenue, where on your left is the south entrance to Baffins Pond.

Benches: In the cemeteries

Picnic Areas: Baffins Pond

Pubs: The Baffins, The Bold Forester, The Festing

Public Toilets: None

Cafes: on Highland Road

Shops: Plenty

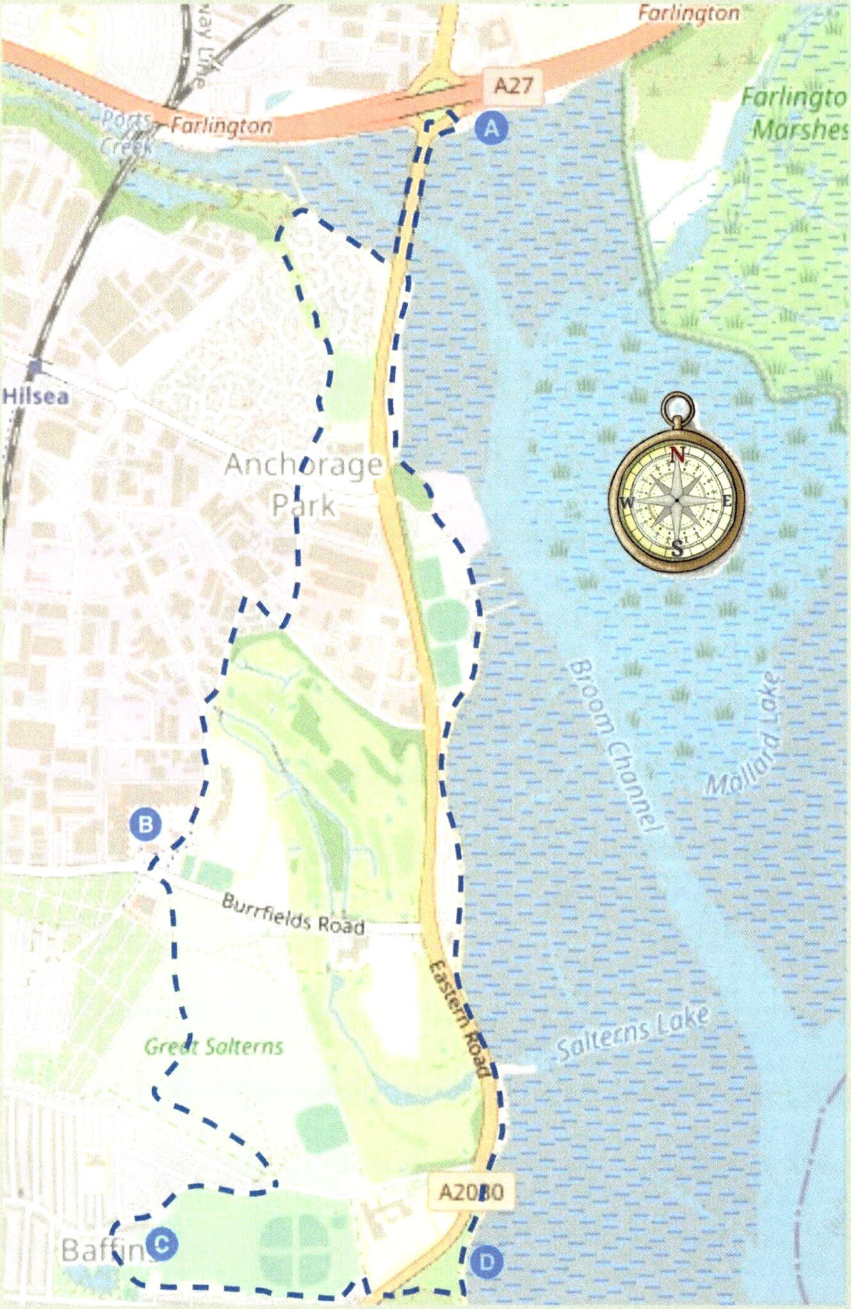
Farlington
A27
Farlington Marshes
Ports Creek
Farlington
A
Hilsea
Anchorage Park
N
W
E
S
Broom Channel
Mallard Lake
B
Burrfields Road
Eastern Road
Great Salterns
Salterns Lake
A2030
C
D
Baffins

P7. Flying By Langstone

6.50 Miles | 2 Hours 30 Mins | 0 Ft Ascent

Gravel Tracks and Pavement

Farlington Marshes (Free), PO6 1SR, Langstone Harbour Viewing Car Park (Free), PO3 6QB, Ocean Retail Park, PO3 35NP

Bus: Morrisons (Hilsea) 21, 621, or Portsmouth College 13, 14, 621

Nearest Train Station: Hilsea (0.25 miles)

This walk takes you along the east shoreline of Portsea Island, with a section inland to cover the site of the old Portsmouth Airport and Baffins Pond. If 6.5 miles is too long there are a couple of shortcuts you can take to reduce the total distance.

I start from the car park at Farlington Marshes, but there are car parks on the Eastern Road (Langstone Harbour Viewing Car Park) or at Ocean Retail Park (PO3 5NP) on this route - at the time of going to print there are no restrictions on any of these car parks. Walking in an anti-clockwise direction, you finish along the shoreline rather than the area which is built up, and the best picnic areas are at the southern end of the walk. Please be careful crossing the Eastern Road as there is a pedestrian crossing at the southern end but only at the northern end if you cross by using the main roundabout just above (towards the hill) the Farlington Marshes car park.

A Leaving the Farlington Marshes car park, head south along the road bridge over Portsbridge Creek until you cross the road at the point where the path from the shore meets the road. Take the yellow gravel path up onto the sea wall, following it through the gate. After the gate, the path cuts back to your left to another gate. Go through, then follow the path through the park all the way to Maidford Grove (crossing two smaller roads). Keep left as the road joins Sywell Crescent and on to Anchorage Road, just past Morrisons ahead of you on your left.

Before reaching the roundabout, cross over to the right-hand side of the road using the pedestrian crossing, then head down Robinson Way, opposite, until it joins the Airport Service Road. Don't cut through the gaps in the hedgerow here as it leads to the golf course which is private property, instead, take a right along Airport Service Road, past Portsmouth Aviation, and then left down Dundas Lane.

The area you are walking through was the site of Portsmouth City Airport (1932-1973). Portsmouth Aviation was formed as the Inland Flying Services in 1929 and in their history the female aviation pioneer Amy Johnson worked for them prior to World War II, and the Portsmouth Aerocar (*right, from The Aeroplane Spotter, 1947*) was designed by them, although only one was ever built. Winston Churchill, then First Lord of the Admiralty, flew into Portsmouth in 1914 - though despite the photos he did not pilot the plane (*main picture*). Churchill did have lessons, and was trying for his pilot's licence, but there was considerable political and personal (his wife) pressure to stop the attempt after several crashes.

B Keep heading along Dundas Lane, past the Admiral Lord Nelson School on your left, until you reach Burrfields Road. The Ocean Retail Park on your right, which opened in the mid 1980's, has various coffee and fast-food places in it if you need refreshments and/or toilets.

If you want a shorter walk, keep heading east along Burrfields Road until you reach the Eastern Road. Crossover, then turn left (heading north) back to the Farlington Marshes car park. This will cut your walk down to four miles in length.

Cross Burrfields Road at the pedestrian crossing, heading left past the office outlet - immediately after the access road for the outlets is a path going through the trees and onto the playing fields.

Follow this path onto Great Salterns Recreation Ground. Keep to the right-hand edge of the field towards the far corner, then left towards the green groundsman's hut by the cricket pitch. Several hundred feet before the hut, you will see a car park and road on your right. Head to the car park, then head down Tangier Road diagonally to your right.

Again, if you wish to shorten your walk, head left at the car park along Tangier Road to get back to the Eastern Road.

C Follow Tangier Road to Baffins Pond (*left)* - the pond itself not the car park (which is the same car park for walk **P6**) - then turn left so the pond is on your right. You can sit on the bench to take in the view or nip over to the Baffins Pub for refreshments. A couple of roads along to the east, Whitecliffe Avenue is built over the remains of a Roman cemetery, though no signs are visible today.

Head south to the tennis courts where there is a path along the left edge, follow this by the side of the field, and then through the trees by the small fence. This brings you out at a set of garages, where a path on your right runs between the houses. Go through and turn left, heading along Hayling Avenue. At the end, just before the Eastern Road, is a newsagent – this is your last chance to get refreshments before heading back to the car park at Farlington Marshes.

Turn right down the Eastern Road to get to the pedestrian crossing, cross, then head back north a few yards until you see the paths heading out onto Milton Common. Take the yellow gravel path to your right rather than the dark tarmac one. Stay on this path, passing the picnic benches, and just after a crossroads in the path there is a turn to your left up a grass/gravel track. Take this until you come to another crossroads with a small bench ahead and take the wider path on the right. Follow this until you reach the gravel service road, where you turn left onto the coastal path.

D Ahead of you is Langstone Harbour, and in the distance is a broken concrete '*Phoenix Breakwater*', which was a section of the Mulberry Harbours built for D-Day in World War II. They were designed to be towed across the Channel and could be flooded (*above*) to sink them in place, forming a semi-permanent harbour structure to unload troops, tanks, and supplies. This one was wrecked before leaving the harbour and has remained in place since.

At the shore, turn left and follow the coastal path all the way back to Farlington Marshes where you started. You will pass Swan Lake and Frog Lake, the People's Memorial - which is a non-affiliated place of remembrance - and then past the Harvester Inn.

Next is the Andrew Simpson Sailing Centre, who do great taster sessions in sailing, windsurfing, and kayaking. In summer Langstone has a population of harbour seals, so the kayaking sessions are well worth trying if you get the chance (they do vouchers which are handy for a birthday present). The last thing of note on this walk is the clump of pine trees just after the sailing centre where you can find giant pinecones in the autumn.

Benches: By Baffin's Pond

Picnic Areas: By Baffin's Pond, or on Milton Common

Pubs: Compass Rose, The Baffins, Great Salterns

Public Toilets: Ocean Retail Park

Cafes: Ocean Retail Park

Shops: Morrisons, Ocean Retail Park, Eastern Road

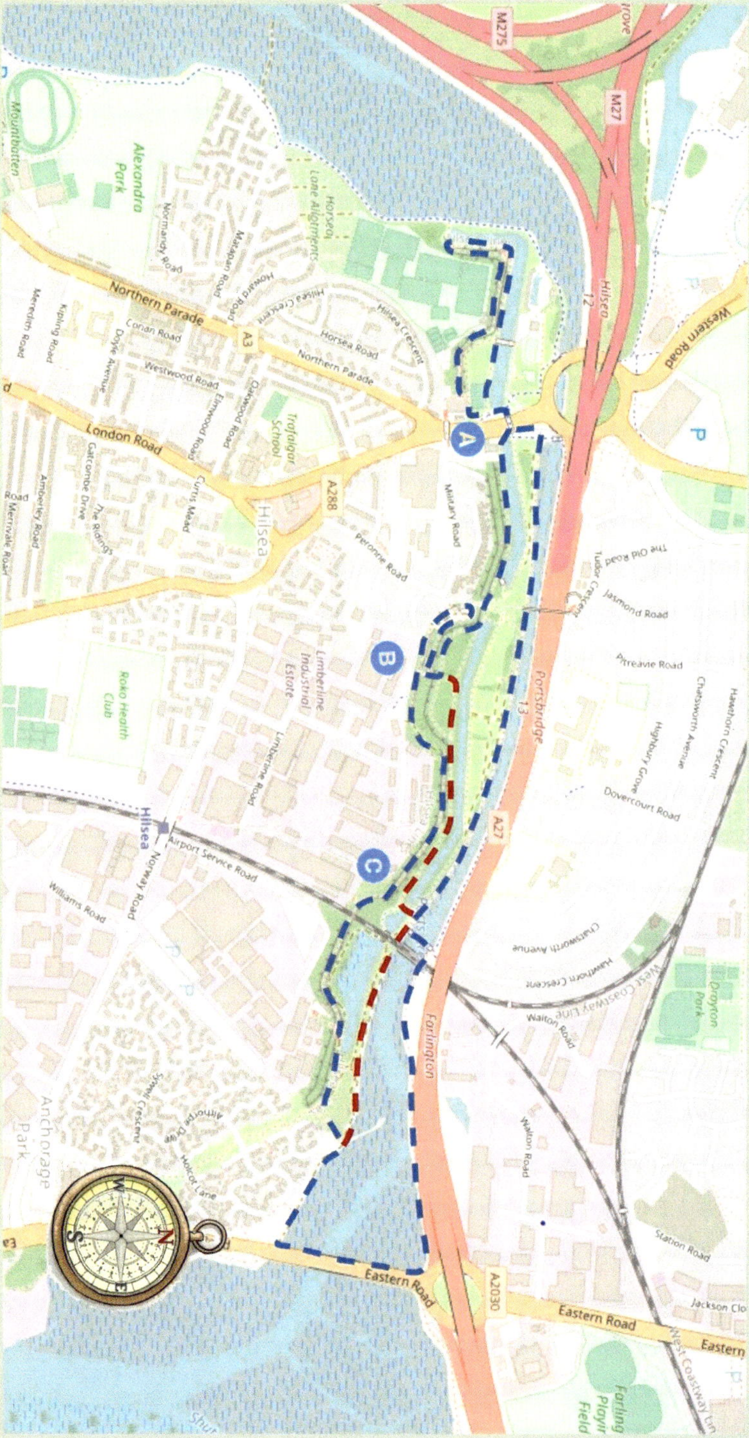
M275
M27
Alexandra Park
Mountbatten
Horsea Lane Allotments
Normandy Road
Maralyn Road
Howard Road
Northern Parade
Hilsea Crescent
Horsea Road
Conan Road
Doyle Avenue
Westwood Road
A3
Oakwood Road
Elmwood Road
Trafalgar School
London Road
A288
Military Road
Peronne Road
Curtis Mead
Hilsea
Meredith Road
Kipling Road
Gatcombe Drive
The Ridings
Amberley Road
Merrivale Road
Roko Health Club
Limberline Industrial Estate
Limberline Road
Airport Service Road
Norway Road
Williams Road
Anchorage Park
Sywell Crescent
Allthorpe Drive
Holcot Lane
Eastern Road
A2030
Portsbridge
A27
Farlington
Hilsea
Western Road
The Old Road
Tudor Crescent
Jasmond Road
Pitreavie Road
Chatsworth Avenue
Hawthorn Crescent
Highbury Grove
Dovercourt Road
West Coastway Line
Walton Road
Drayton Park
Station Road
Jackson Clo
Farling Playi Field
A
B
C
N
S
E
W

P8. The Hilsea Lines

4.25 Miles | 1 Hour 30 Mins | 41 Ft Ascent

Pavement, Track, Forest Path

Parking: Hilsea (Free), PO2 9RR, alternate Farlington Marshes (Free), PO6 1SR

Bus: Hilsea Lido, 2, 3, 8, 20, 700

Nearest Train Station: Cosham, Hilsea (.5 Miles)

Like Creech Wood and the Meon Valley Trail, there are different paths you can take to explore Hilsea Lines. However, please remember the area is a scheduled ancient monument so keep to the paths rather than scramble up and down the banks, as tempting as it is! There is a great history guide you can print off for the Lines if you search the internet for '*Hilsea Lines Military Leaflet*' and check the notice boards in the area for the walks the Hilsea Lines Wardens run in the area.

This route takes you from one end of the Lines to the other, as well as round to the North bank of Portsbridge Creek, but please keep an eye on the tide levels as if it is a middle to high tide there is one section that is not accessible (an alternative route is provided, check the King's Harbour Master website in advance for the Portsmouth tide times). Also, there is a long section that follows the path along the top of the bastions which can become overgrown. If you prefer not to have to push the occasional branch aside, I have suggested an easier route.

The railway lines into Portsmouth have an unusual history, in that they were both delayed and had their route dictated by these fortifications (and the ones around Old Portsmouth). Whilst Gosport had their railway line in place by 1841 (after much discussion as the navy board felt it came too close to the fortifications on that side of the harbour), it was another six years before Portsmouth had theirs. Despite the requirements of the dockyard for a direct goods line, the thought of breaching Hilsea Lines to allow a railway through was unacceptable for many years.

A Starting from the car park by the old Evening News Centre, cross the A3 using the concrete bridge so you are heading west towards the Lido and take the path so the skate park is on your left. Head past the wakeboarding towers (you can see wakeboarders practicing here at the weekends) and round the corner until you come to the end. Behind you to the left are a set of stairs heading up onto the bastion. Take these and follow until the path splits into three. You can take either the left or middle paths, both bring you back to the concrete bridge. Cross back over the bridge, taking the gravel path immediately in front of you that leads to the main section of the fortifications (so the lake is on your right).

These fortifications, collectively known as the Hilsea Lines, were built in two main phases from 1756 and from 1851, being fully completed in 1871. They were designed to protect Portsea Island from inland attacks but were obsolete before they were completed, as advances in artillery range and accuracy meant that an inland force could bombard the dockyard and associated infrastructure from the other side of Portsdown Hill.

Follow the path until you come to the road, cross, then take the path that leads into the woods (so the lake is now on your left). Keep right as you pass the woodland classroom until you reach a tunnel through the brickwork on your right. If it is spring, there will be an abundance of bluebells and wild garlic (*above*).

B Go through the tunnel, turn right, and keep going until you reach a clear view of the bastions with a few picnic benches (*opposite, bottom*) . You now have a decision to make: If you want to take the *'explorer's path'*, head up the slope to the left of the bastions and follow it as it curves back along the top of them. Stay on this path, crossing the railway bridge, until you reach the far end of the fortifications. As I mentioned, you may have to push some branches out of the way, but stay on the path following the fence. When the fence finishes, keep straight on, taking a left when you reach a T-junction with a tree in the middle, then straight on until you reach a set of steps on the left. If you want to visit the World War 1 Remembrance Centre (**highly recommended – see Page 147**), then at the T-junction with the tree turn right and head to Bastion Number 6.

MONCRIEFF GUN CARRIAGE

If you do not want to take this path, and would prefer a more open track, then go back through the tunnel, turning right when you come out of it, and take this woodland track all the way to the Eastern Road.

At its height, there were over 150 guns mounted along these fortifications, and in 1875 several of the 'new' Moncrieff disappearing guns were installed (*above*). Weighing in at around 7 tons each, these guns were designed to be loaded whilst they were lowered in their protective pit, they could then be raised to be fired, with the recoil forcing them back down into the pit again, giving the crews protection whilst they were reloaded.

C When you get a clear view of Portsbridge Creek and the railway bridge, **take a note of the water levels**. If you continue all the way round, there is a path that goes under the railway bridge, which is inaccessible at mid to high tide (*above*). If the tide is high, cross the footbridge to the left of the railway bridge, taking you to the northern bank, then turn left and head back round to the car park (this also reduces your route by about a mile-and-a-half).

If the tide is low, then continue to the Eastern Road, turn left and walk along the bridge to the main roundabout, where you will see a path on the left heading back along the northern bank of the creek. Take this path until you reach the railway bridge with the path running underneath it. Go through, and on the other side you come to a footbridge. Cross back over the creek and turn right. Follow this wide track to the road, cross, then take the path to the left, taking you back to the main car park where you started.

Benches: Plenty

Picnic Areas: Several picnic benches along the route

Pubs: Coach and Horses, the Compass Rose, within 10 minutes of the path

Public Toilets: Hilsea Public Toilets

Cafes: Hilsea Lines Cafe, Kemals, Casemates Coffee Hut

Shops: Shell Garage

A
B
C
D
Southsea
Portsmouth
Portland Road
Queens Crescent
Grove Road South
Avenue De Caen
Clarence Parade
Auckland Road East
Clarendon Road
B2151
Clarence Esplanade
South Parade
Malvern Road
Victoria Road South
Worthing Road
Exmouth Road
Duncan Road
Napier Road
Albert Road
Albert Grove
Chelsea Road
Goodwood Road
Oxford Road
Boulton Road
Harold Road
Beach Road
Somerset Road
St Simon's Road
Collingwood Road
B2155
Waverley Road
Allen's Road
Gains Road
B2154
Parkstone Avenue
Bembridge Crescent
St Ronan's Road
A288
St Helens Parade
Craneswater Avenue
Craneswater Park
Northcote Road
Wheatstone Road
Bath Road
Festing Road
Saint Augustine Road
Brompton Road
Helena Road
Bruce Road
Salisbury Road
Exeter Road
Bristol Road
Highland Road
Haslemere Road
Mini Golf
Esplanade
Festing Grove
Highland Cemetery
Eastern Parade
Cousins Grove
Burbidge Grove
Brading Avenue
Kimberley Road
Hunter Road
Oliver Road
Eastney Pitch and Putt
Selsey Avenue
Lindley Avenue
Collins Road
Ward Road
Owen Street
St George

P9. One for the Kids (both small and large!)

2.5 Miles | 1 Hour (+ play time) | 16 Ft Ascent

Pavement and Beach

Parking: Seafront Parking (Pay, £5.20 for 4 hours), PO4 0ST

Bus: Canoe Lake 1,23

Nearest Train Station: Fratton (1.4 Miles), Portsmouth and Southsea (2 Miles)

This walk covers the key recreation areas around Canoe Lake and the pier, but does pass various features that charge (as well as free ones), so if you have excitable kids you may want to warn them they won't be able to do everything.

Starting at the bus stop at Canoe Lake, stand with your back to the lake and look up St Helen's Road to the right where you will see Granada Road, between St. Helen's Court and a red brick building with a turret. Head down

A Granada Road until you reach the roundabout to find the large *'Strand Map Mural'* of Portsmouth (*left*), by the artist Mark E.W. Lewis. You may recognise some of Portsmouth's more famous current residents on the map!

Behind you is Burgoyne Road, head down there until you reach South Parade Road, with a zebra crossing just to your right. Cross into the ornamental gardens and walk through the middle of both sets, bringing you out directly across from the Pyramids Centre.

B To the left of the Pyramids is a bench and a path. Take this until you reach the fountain (*below*). You are now in Southsea Rock Gardens and can take your time to explore the paths and the flowers here; when you are ready you want to end up on the seafront promenade.

Take the seafront path and head towards the pier (east). You pass one of the better fish-and-chip places on your left (*The Briny*), and if the weather is warm there will be ice-cream and snack concessions along here as well. When you reach the pier, take the metal stairs up on the outside (if the tide is very high you can use the first turning inside to reach the same place) and head to the end.

If it is out of season (i.e., cold and wet) there will be little to do outside, though there are arcades inside as well as snack-bars and a restaurant. If the weather is decent, there are children's rides, candy-floss stores, and more at the end. For the rides, the tokens cost around £11 for 25, with each ride costing between 5 and 8 tokens per child.

The pier was constructed between 1875 and 1878 to allow the ferries to and from the Isle of Wight to dock. Just 25 years later, in 1904, it was destroyed by fire, and was only rebuilt at 600 feet long, half the original length, re-opening in 1908. It was used to help embark troops for D-Day in 1944, before another fire destroyed the theatre on it in 1966. The third, and most famous fire, was in 1974 when the pier caught fire during the filming of the rock-opera film *'Tommy'*.

When you are ready, carry on along the seafront and you want the third zebra crossing, which is just after Southsea Model Village and faces the entrance to the Rose Gardens. The Rose Gardens are

C actually built in the remains of Lumps Fort, which we know existed in 1805 but is believed to date back to a circular redoubt from 1545. There is also a small Japanese garden off to the eastern side as well, which marks the twinning of Portsmouth with the Japanese city of Maizuru in 1998.

In 1942, before it became the Rose Gardens, it was used as the training centre for Operation Frankton, where ten Royal Marines used five kayaks launched from the submarine *HMS Tuna* to attack ships in Bordeaux harbour, though only two kayaks reached the harbour. They managed to damage six ships, but only two of the Royal Marines survived the operation. It was the basis of the film, *The Cockleshell Heroes (1955)*, some of which was filmed at the old Eastney barracks.

Take a stroll through the Rose Gardens (*main picture*), and the Japanese Gardens if you so desire, then exit opposite where you entered, heading left, alongside the mini-golf course. If it is open, the mini-golf charges £3 per person for a few holes.

Optional: Just after the mini golf, on the left, is the path that leads to Southsea Model Village (*above*). The Village opened in 1956 and is set to 1/12th scale. It is £5 for adults, £4 for concessions, with a family ticket available too. Though not large, everyone should go once, especially with the Rifleman's Tunnel to visit and the mound to climb to reach the castle. Some of the model trains running in the village are Thomas the Tank Engine themed, and youngsters can get a free quiz on entry to take round with them.

D Back on the main path, there is a large play-area on the left, which can get very busy in peak summer hours, but has plenty to keep the kids amused. Once you have tried to tire them out, carry on towards the Canoe Lake Café, where just before it on the right should be an open gate signposted '*Cumberland House*'. Go through the gardens and into Cumberland House itself. The building is free to visit – though please donate if you can – and was purchased for the city in 1928, opening as a museum in 1931. The new butterfly house attached to the building was opened in 2017, and if you visit several times between May and September you will experience different species flying around you (*like this glasswing butterfly, right*). The museum is a great place to learn about the geology and fauna of Portsea Island, and of course is topped off with the huge Emily the Iguanodon. Though she may appear dated to modern dinosaur models, she has a special place in the hearts of most kids who have grown up in Portsmouth.

Leaving Cumberland House, turn left and head back to Canoe Lake, taking the main path back to the café. You can now spend some time with the ducks and swans of Canoe Lake, and this would be a good time to practice your crabbing skills (again, this is one for the checklist of growing up in Portsmouth). For crabbing, you need a bucket (with lake water in it to keep your crabs alive), a net to pull your captures out of the water, a crab line, and some bait. A crab line is a piece of fishing line with a weight on to keep the bait at the bottom of the lake – you should not need to use a hook. Bacon is pretty good to use as bait, and when you drop your line in you must be patient as the crabs have to smell the bait and then walk to it. Use your net to put them in the bucket and remember to change the water in the bucket regularly and release them unharmed before you leave.

Once you have finished around the lake, head back to the bus stops towards the pier.

Benches: Plenty

Picnic Areas: Around Canoe Lake

Pubs: Coach and Horses, The Compass Rose, within 10 minutes of the path

Public Toilets: The Pier, Canoe Lake

Cafes: Plenty

Shops: Co-op opposite the pier

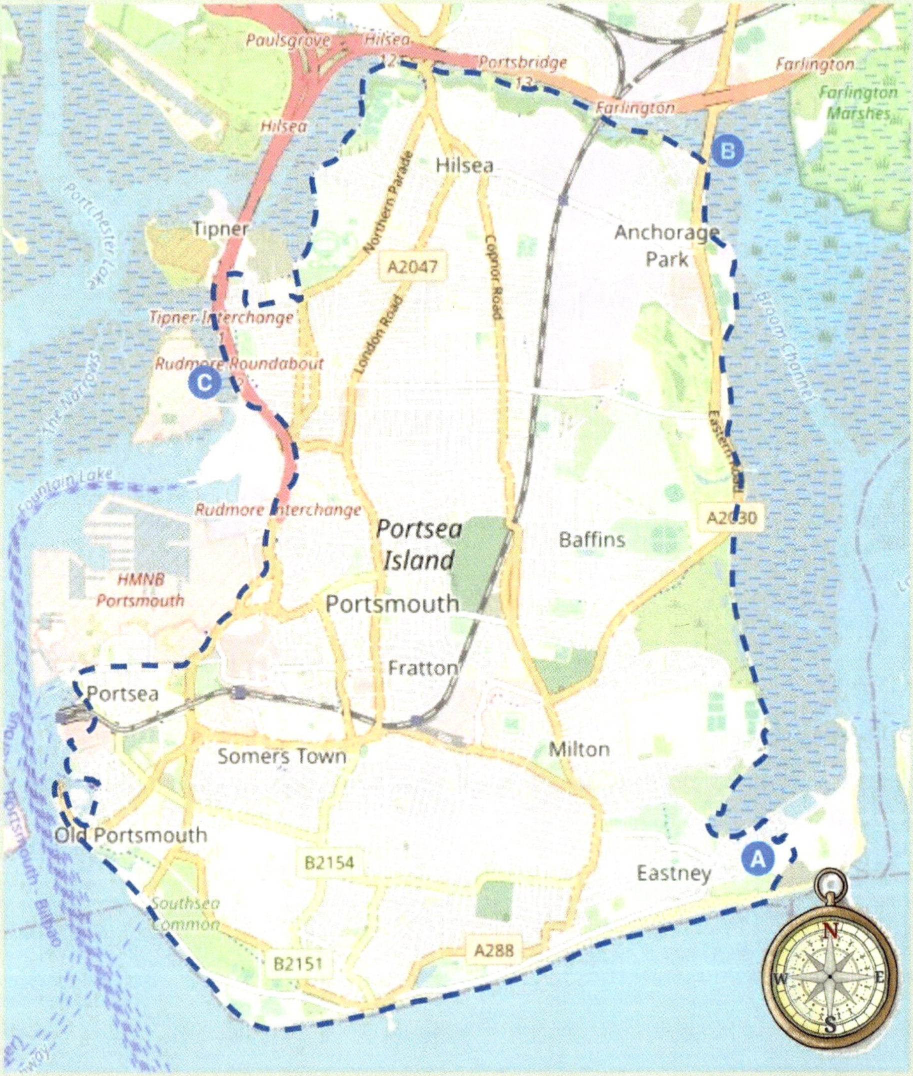

Paulsgrove
Hilsea
12
Portsbridge
13
Farlington
Farlington
Farlington Marshes
Hilsea
B
Portchester Lake
Tipner
Hilsea
Northern Parade
A2047
Copnor Road
Anchorage Park
Tipner Interchange
London Road
Broom Channel
Rudmore Roundabout
C
The Narrows
Eastern Road
Fountain Lake
Rudmore Interchange
A2030
Portsea Island
Baffins
HMNB Portsmouth
Portsmouth
Fratton
Portsea
Somers Town
Milton
Old Portsmouth
B2154
Eastney
A
Southsea Common
A288
B2151
N
W
E
S

P10. The Loop

14.5 Miles 5 Hours 30 Mins 47 Ft Ascent

Pavement, Beach, Trail

Parking: Gunwharf, PO1 3TZ

Bus: The Hard, Hilsea Bus Station

Nearest Train Station: The Hard, Cosham (.5 miles)

Now you've walked sections of Portsea Island, it is time to walk the whole coast! At just under 15 miles in length, find the nearest coast path and walk round until you reach your starting point. There are plenty of pubs, cafes, and refreshment points along the way, and there are some toilet stops available.

Unfortunately, there are a couple of places where the path is not continuous (if you are reading this Portsmouth City Council then please look at joining the route up nicely!) so there are a couple of places where you have to walk inland a bit.

Anti-Clockwise: Starting at the dockyard gates, follow the Millennium Trail (walk **P2**) to Southsea Castle, then stay on the promenade until you reach the public toilets at Eastney (by the swimming baths). Stay on the beach, passing the caravans, until you see an alleyway on your left. This leads to an open area (part of Fort Cumberland) which you cross diagonally to bring you out at the junction of Fort Cumberland Road and Ferry Road.

A If you want to add an extra mile to your journey – and be a completist – walk to the end of Eastney on your right and then back to this junction. Walk through the housing estate until you reach the coast path and follow this to the right. At low tide you can use the beach, at high tide stay on the grass and then take the path behind the allotments to bring you out on Locksway Road. Head to The Thatched House Pub, cross over the old entrance to the Portsmouth and Arundel Canal, then stay on the coastal path all the way to the Eastern Road Bridge (just before Farlington Marshes).

B Cross the Eastern Road and go west along the Hilsea Lines, following it round (*above*) until you reach the Mountbatten Centre. Here you need to do a bit of roadwork. Come out of the gardens of the Mountbatten Centre at the roundabout opposite '*The Avenue*' (where the A3 meets Twyford Avenue) and take the first right, Tipner Road. This turns into Tipner Lane as it bends to the right, then C head left when it reaches the Park and Ride car park. Cross the roundabout under the M275, and the path continues on your left (and you are back on the coast path).

This will take you to an underpass on your left, by HMS Excellent on Whale Island, which leads to multiple exits under the Rudmore Roundabout. The south-east exit brings you out alongside the old Admiral Drake pub. Continue south until the crossing point which takes you back to the other side of the A3 and the M275 by the ferry port (you can take the south-west exit from under the Rudmore Roundabout, but you have to walk alongside the ferry port road so this way is safer).

Walk past Morrisons, down Hope Street and Alfred Road (past St. John's Cathedral), and finally down Queen Street and back to the dockyard gates where you started. All you need to do now is pop into the Ship and Castle for a well-deserved drink and a bite to eat.

Most of this route is doable on a bicycle, with the exceptions around Eastney. When you reach the public toilets and the old Eastney Swimming Pool, cycle up Henderson Road, left onto Bransbury Road, and then right up Milton Road. When you reach the mini roundabout take Locksway Road to the right.

If I manage to sell a few copies of this book, I'll look at putting together a certificate, badge, or something similar that people can apply for to show that they have completed the route – please check my website or Facebook page (www.ajnoon.com or @ajnoon).

Portchester, just off Portsea Island, was one of the earliest inhabited settlements in the area, with prehistoric and Mesolithic flints having been found along the shoreline. It can be considered the original heart of Portsmouth, with 20 households recorded here in the Domesday Book of 1086. By comparison, Fratton had 12 households, Buckland 10, and Copnor 9.

The earliest remains of the Roman fort, *Portus Adurni*, date to the 3rd Century, and from the 11th Century it was developed into the structure you can visit now. The castle grounds were used to house prisoners of war during many conflicts, including the Anglo-Dutch Wars (1660's), the French Revolutionary Wars (1792 – 1802), and the Napoleonic Wars (1803 – 1815), with buildings to imprison up to 8,000 men constructed inside the walls. Most of these buildings no longer remain, however the Church of St. Mary is still here which was built in the 1120's.

The village of Southwick is based around the remains of an old priory, which was moved from the grounds of Portchester Castle sometime between 1145 and 1153. The priory was then dismantled in 1538 during Henry VIII's Dissolution of the Monasteries, and it then became known as Southwick Park.

Little remains of the priory now, but just to the north-east of the monastery site sits Southwick House, built in 1800, which is known for the role it played during World War II. It is from here that the final preparations were made for D-Day, and you can see the original planning room and D-Day maps in place.

Denmead was once owned by the Bishop of Winchester, becoming a manor in 1449. The land was split up over the years into smaller parcels, until it became its own parish in 1880. During World War II the woods in the area were used to provide cover for the gathering D-Day troops, and prisoners of war were also kept there.

Queen Elizabeth Country Park is the largest park in the area, covering over 1,400 acres, with the South Downs Way passing through it (Winchester to Eastbourne, 100 miles). Butser Hill, the highest point on the South Downs, comes in at 885 feet high and is the second highest point in Hampshire (the highest is Pilot Hill, the *'County Top'* near Highclere, at 938 feet). QE Country Park opened in 1975 and has fields, forest, and downs to explore. There are numerous trails for walking and cycling, picnic areas (including designated BBQ sites), and a café. It is a great area for orienteering, frisbees, walking the dog, and kite-flying.

Butser Ancient Farm (*below*) is close to Queen Elizabeth Country Park and well worth a visit, especially in spring for the new-born lambs and kids of the speciality breeds they house there. The site, opened in 1970, is a centre for experimental archaeology and has reconstructions of buildings and skills from the Stone Age up to the Anglo-Saxon period on display. NB: If you do visit, they use open fires for heating and lighting, so your clothes will pick up the odours. Butser is very popular for school visits, and they run their own Beltain festival as well as regular crafting workshops. Visiting costs are around £10 per adult and £6 per child, with a family ticket available and a yearly membership option.

Kenwood Road
Bayly Avenue
Roman Grove Allotments
Fareham
Wicor Path
Hospital Lane
Waterside Lane
Castle Street
The Keep
Castle Trading Estate
Castle Shore Open Space
East Street
Southampton Road
A27
Portchester Lake
Paulsgrove Lake
Horsea Island Country Park
Marina Keep
Lock View
Port Way
Newlyn Way
Port Solent
Paulsgrove
12
Horsea Island (Defence
A
B
C
P

N1. Portchester Castle

5.25 Miles | 1 Hour 45 Mins | 45 Ft Ascent

Pavement, gravel track, field boundary path

Parking: Port Solent, PO6 4TP (free), Portchester Castle (£1 per hour), PO16 9QW

Bus: Portchester Precinct, 3, X4

Nearest Train Station: Portchester (.15 Miles)

This walk combines two loops taking you around Port Solent and Portchester Castle. It gives great views into Paulsgrove Lake, out across Portchester Lake, and then towards the main harbour mouth. To the south you should see Spinnaker Tower, maybe an aircraft carrier or two (*right*) and, weather conditions permitting, the Isle of Wight. To the north are the forts up on Portsdown Hill. There are a couple of decent picnic areas on the walk, one at Port Solent and one inside the castle grounds, but I'd recommend taking blankets to sit on as benches are sparse.

You can start this walk either by Portchester Castle or at Port Solent, and although there are two stretches of road, one takes the coastal path and the other takes you through heart of Portchester, which has some amazing buildings still present.

A Starting at the main gates of Portchester Castle (*left*), take Castle Street away from the castle heading north towards Portchester Precinct. Follow Castle Street all the way to the main roundabout by Portchester Precinct, passing over 30 listed buildings on this one road - keep an eye out for the blue plaques as you walk. If you fancy a Sunday lunch, then the Cormorant Pub do very good roasts (at time of going to print).

When you reach the roundabout, with the Red Lion to your left, head right (east) along the A27 towards Cosham. You pass some fairly standard houses but keep an eye on the other side of the road for the large white building, the 18th Century Murrills House. This building is Grade II listed and was built on a farm site dating back to 1500, when it was surrounded by over 200 acres of grazing land! On your right, just after Mother Kelly's fish and chip restaurant and the garage, is a path running parallel to the road taking you along the sea wall.

Looking up to Portsdown Hill, two large grey structures are visible, and if you know your Royal Navy ships you will note that the left one is a replica of a Type 23 frigate's superstructure, and the right that of a Type 45 destroyer (*right*). The systems are run by several of the Royal Navy suppliers and are used for testing the radars and sensors fitted onto their ships.

B Continue along the sea wall, and when you reach Lock View turn right to the lock gates of Port Solent. This development was built on reclaimed land - the hill behind Port Solent was the old council tip – and was officially opened in 1988. Cross along the top of the lock gates - you may have to wait for a yacht to pass through – and continue following the coastal path until you reach the fenced off compound that is part of HMS Excellent.

Here, after admiring the view of Portchester Castle on your right, turn left and follow the path by the southern edge of the field. The path by the fence is sometimes closed so, if it is, cross the stile and follow the field edge. Behind the fence is the Defence Diving School and part of HMS Excellent (the Naval Headquarters based on Whale Island).

The field you are crossing makes a good picnic or frisbee area, and there is a solitary picnic bench towards the far tree line (nearest the small hill). The path follows the fence, so stick to it until it curves to your left through the small trees and up the gentle hill. Keep on this path until you come to the entrance to Port Solent Country Park, which hopefully will be open by the time you are reading this. If it is, then feel free to explore the park, otherwise continue by taking the path down to your left. Cross the road at the car park, and head into Port Solent.

Take the stairs down to the left of the cinema, through the glass doors, and then onto the Boardwalk, where you turn left and the marina path takes you back to the lock gates. If the weather is calm, you should see plenty of large fish in the shadows by the boats and pontoons, and just after the end of the Boardwalk you can find a children's play area and public toilets.

Go back over the lock gates, up Lock View and back along the A27 the way you came until you reach Hamilton Road, half-way between Mother Kelly's and the main roundabout at Portchester. Turn left down Hamilton Road making your way to the large drums you see at the end. You may notice the drums slowly turning as they produce subsea carbon fibre pipes.

C To the right of the drums is a public footpath which leads back to Portchester Castle, where you can walk around the outside of the walls until you reach the entrance where you started. As you pass the southern walls, look up to see the 12th Century garderobe chutes (toilets) still present.

It is free to enter the grounds of the castle, and they make a great picnic spot. There is usually a small coffee and cake van present as well as the tearooms in St. Mary's Church (the church was built in the 1120's). The grounds and keep are maintained by English Heritage, and to enter the keep itself costs around £9 for adults and £5 for children (family tickets are available).

If you have an interest in naval history, buried at the church are three gentlemen of note: James Lind, who worked in areas including fumigation of ship's holds, distillation of fresh water from seawater, and the use of fresh fruit to help prevent scurvy. Thomas Goble, who was onboard *HMS Victory* at the Battle of Trafalgar serving as a master's mate, though he took on John Scott's role of Secretary of the Fleet when Scott was killed during the battle. The third grave of interest if that of William Lionel Wyllie, a renowned maritime artist. Wyllie was instrumental in the campaign for the saving and restoration of *HMS Victory* at the start of the 20th century.

Keep an eye on the walls inside the keep if you visit to see if you can find any of the graffiti from when it was used as a prisoner-of-war camp. Also, In the north-east corner of the car park behind the bushes, is the old gunpowder store from 1850.

There should be plenty of wildlife to see on this walk, especially if you do this at low tide (check the King's Harbour Master website for tide times). Little Egrets (*above*) are relatively new to the UK, with the first record of them breeding here in 1996, but you can now see them in the coastal margins all around Portsmouth.

Benches: Around the castle and overlooking Paulsgrove Lake

Picnic Areas: 2, the castle and Port Solent.

Pubs: Two in Portchester and two in Port Solent

Public Toilets: Port Solent

Cafes: At the castle and Port Solent

Shops: Port Solent

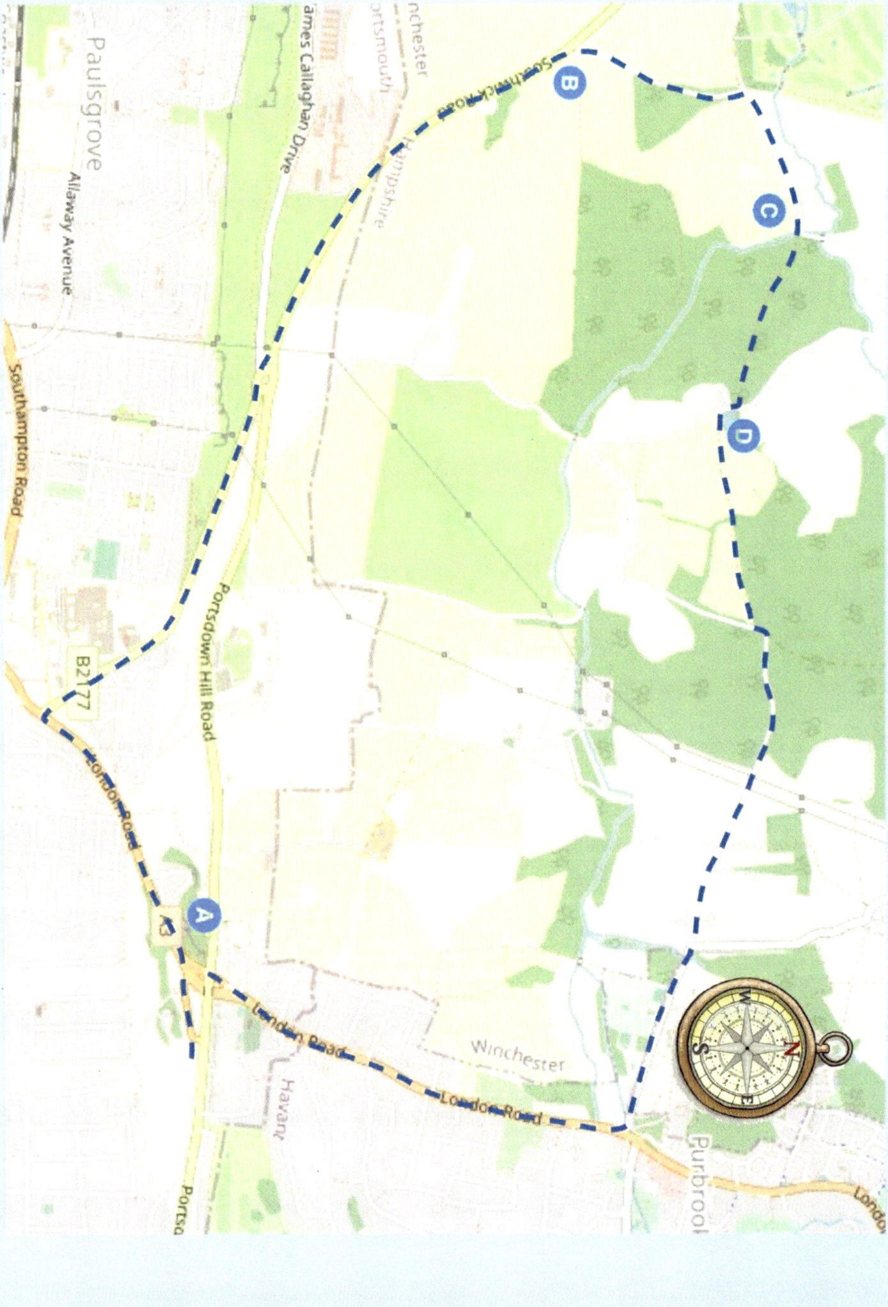
Paulsgrove
Allaway Avenue
Southampton Road
James Callaghan Drive
Hampshire
Southwick Road
Portsdown Hill Road
B2177
London Road
A3
Havant
Winchester
Purbrook
A
B
C
D
N
E
S
W

N2. Portsdown Hill Front and Back

6.5 Miles | 3 Hours | 574 Ft Ascent

Pavement, road, track

Parking: Portsdown Hill, PO6 1BG (free), or by Churchillian Pub, PO6 3LS (free)

Bus: The George Inn, 7, 7C, SC5

Nearest Train Station: Cosham (1 Mile)

This walk, though it has some sections along roads, serves several purposes. Firstly, it gives great views both from - and of - Portsdown Hill, and secondly it helps to show you where various paths link up, such as the Wayfarer's Trail and the Pilgrim's Trail.

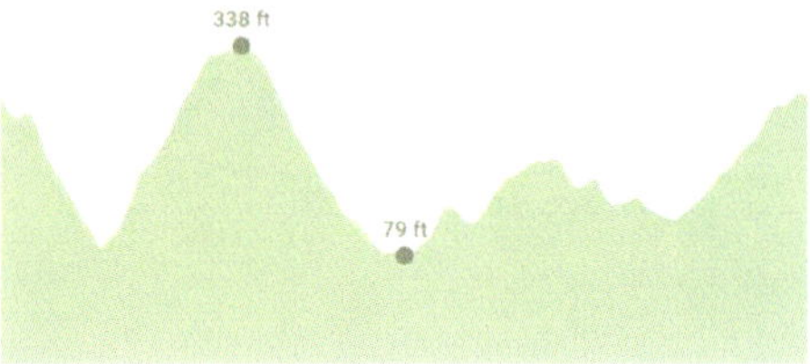

Starting from the Pilgerruh car park, head west until you reach London Road and follow it down (so the George Inn is on your right).

A You may notice the dense clump of trees on your right as you head down, if you are feeling adventurous you can head into these to find the cave there carved out of the chalk that makes up Portsdown Hill (*left*).

When you reach the traffic lights - before Cosham High Street – turn right up Southwick Hill Road so you are passing Queen Alexandra Hospital on your left. When the path on the right runs out, cross over and carry on up the hill on the left-hand side of the road (do not take the path on the right up into the trees).

Queen Alexandra Hospital was originally built as a military hospital and opened in 1908. In 1926 it was re-designated to cater for ex-servicemen, before being incorporated into the NHS in 1951. It still has strong ties with the military, especially with the Royal Navy, and it is not uncommon to be treated there by serving personnel.

At the top of the hill you reach a roundabout, take the road diagonally opposite from you (signposted '*Southwick*') which takes you past the Portsdown Technology Park where various radars and sensors are tested for the Royal Navy - which is why one of the radar set-ups looks like a Type 45 Destroyer and the smaller set-up resembles a Type 23 Frigate.

B When you come to the lodge on the right hand-side, take Pitymoor Lane (not the footpath across the field). There is no pavement for this section but the road is quiet so you should not be too inconvenienced. At the bottom of the lane it bends to the right, which you follow, but note on your left the footpath alongside the old monastery boundary walls. This footpath is part of the Pilgrim's Trail (Winchester to Portsmouth) and leads to Southwick if you want a drink in one of the pubs there.

C Heading east on Pitymoor Lane there is still no pavement, but after passing Comphouse Farm you come to a bend in the road. On the right is a path into the woods (not the gate) which you need to take (*opposite bottom*). You now have a nice stroll through Sawyer's Wood, following the signs, until you come to Pigeon House Lane.

D Turn right to the farm, then take the stile over the gate opposite the farm on your left. Follow the path through the field to the far end, where you go up the bank, then come out into another field (*main picture*). Cross this field and the next, then you reach another road.

Again, for the first section there is no pavement to walk on until halfway along.

When you reach the tennis courts on your right, there is the Rowans Hospice on your left, and you are now on a section of walk **N3**. For this walk go straight ahead until you reach London Road (the A3), where in front of you is a bakery and a fish and chip shop if you want refreshments. Head up the hill (to your right) until you reach the George Inn (*below*).

When the area around the Inn was dug out for the road cuttings, a Neolithic long barrow (with human remains inside) was excavated, and the present inn dates back to the late 18th Century. There are strong indications there was an inn at the same site prior to the current building and it is said they used to hold auctions and even inquests at the inn.

Buzzards (*left*) and red kites are becoming a common sight on the hill, with both being large raptors. Buzzards have rounded wingtips and tails, whereas red kits have a forked tail. Red kites were heavily hunted, being blamed for taking lambs, and at one point they were confined to Wales. In the early 1990's a breeding programme was setup and in the last couple of years they have been regular visitors in summer around Fort Nelson and Southwick.

Take the opportunity for a well-earned drink at the George, then head back to the car park where you started to your left.

Benches: At the top of Portsdown Hill

Picnic Areas: Top of the hill, and Purbrook Heath Recreation Ground

Pubs: The George Inn

Public Toilets: None

Cafes: Purbrook, after the Rowans Hospice

Shops: Purbrook

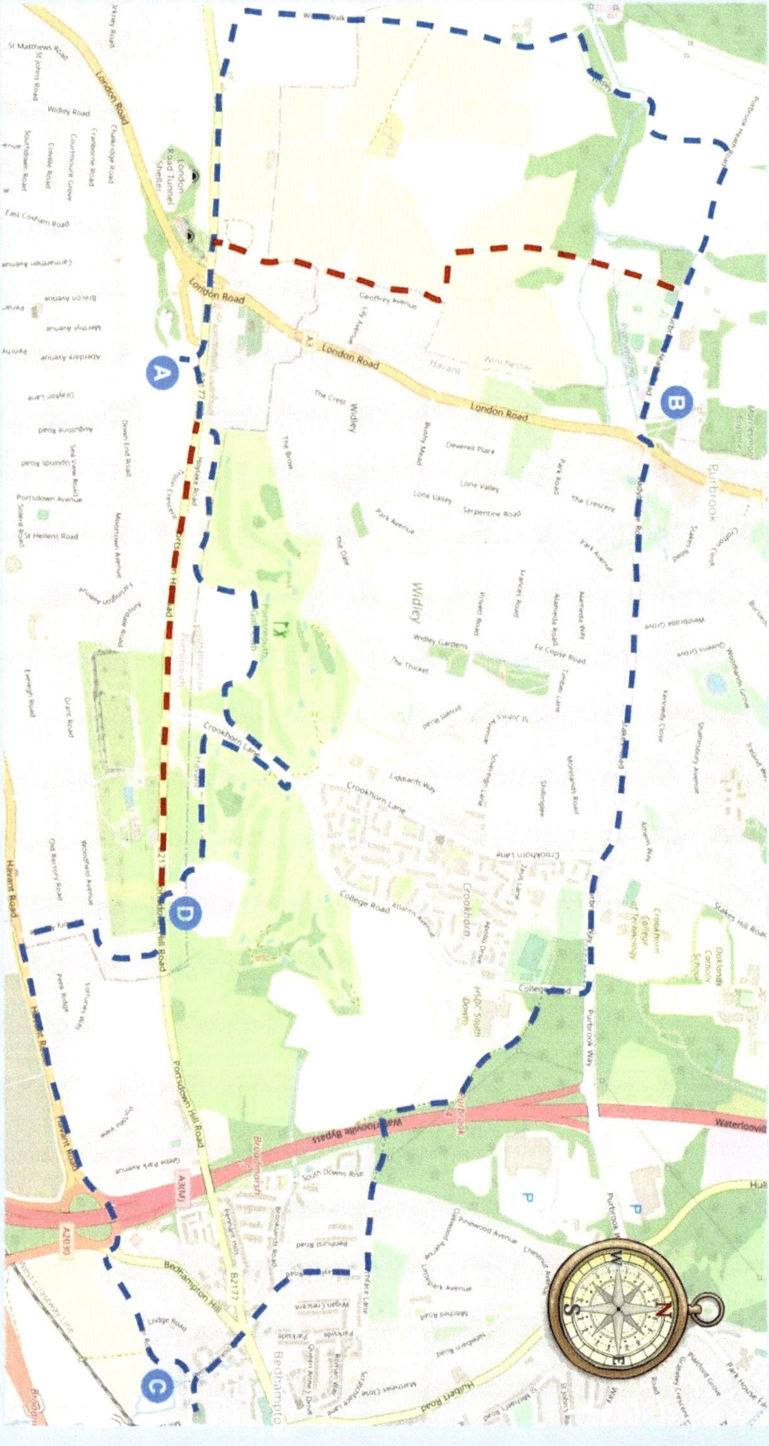
A
B
C
D
London Road
London Road Tunnel Shelter
Geoffrey Avenue
Widley
Portsmouth Golf Club
Crookhorn Lane
Crookhorn
College Road
Purbrook Way
Purbrook
Waterlooville Bypass
A3(M)
A2030
Havant Road
Portsdown Hill Road
Bedhampton Hill
B2177
Hulbert Road
Bedhampton
Lodge Road
Stakes Hill Road
Crookhorn College of Technology
Oaklands Catholic School
HSDC South Downs

N3. Portsdown Hill Circular (with added trees)

8.25 Miles | 3 Hours | 530 Ft Ascent

Pavement, Gravel, Trackway

Parking: Portsdown Hill, PO6 1BG (free), or by Churchillian Pub, PO6 3LS (free)

Bus: The George Inn, 7, 7C, SC5

Nearest Train Station: Cosham (1 Mile)

This walk takes you along the top of Portsdown Hill, down to Purbrook, along to Crookhorn, through Bedhampton, and then back to the top of the hill. Portsmouth only has one proper hill, so if anyone says *'the hill'*, they mean Portsdown Hill. There is a section of this walk that goes through urban areas in Purbrook and Bedhampton, but it passes the two oldest trees in the area, one of which is over 600 years old and may even be closer to 900 years old. There are also several shortcuts you can take on this route if 8.5 miles is not what you are looking for, and it is easy to drop up to 2.5 miles.

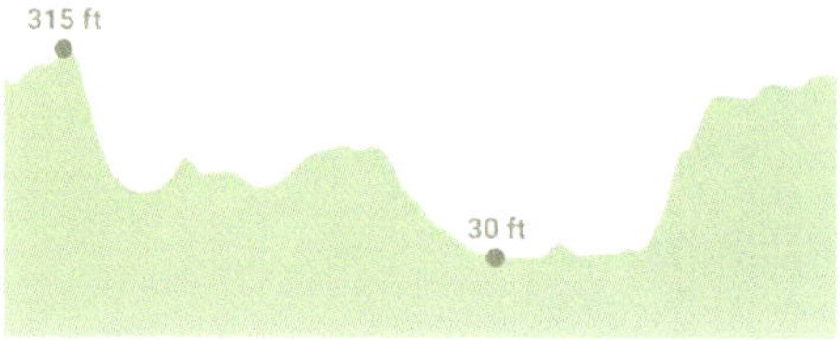

A Starting at the Pilgerruh public car park (PO6 3LS), head west along the top of Portsdown Hill, passing the George Inn on your right.

If you want to take a mile off the route, take Dellcrest Path on your right, which takes you down to the tennis courts by the Rowans Hospice. This will reduce the walk by a mile, but the first part of this path can be overgrown so is not ideal if you are wearing shorts. Follow this path to the end of the houses, where it turns to the left, and keep following until it turns to the right again, so you are heading north. Stay on this path until you reach the tennis courts, where you turn right to the Rowan's Hospice.

You will come to *'Mick's Monster Burgers'*, renowned in Portsmouth, and an ice-cream van is often here when the weather is good. There are some great views of Portsmouth to be had from here (*main picture*), as well as being a prime play area for frisbees and kites. On the grass verge on the opposite side of the main road, to the right of Harbour Heights, is a memorial to Hubert Adair, a Hurricane pilot who was shot down here in 1940 (*left*).

Just after the food vans and parking, is a clump of beech trees, 255 of them in fact, and they were planted in 1982 in remembrance of the British losses (both military and civilian) during the Falklands Conflict of that year.

Cross over the road at the top of the hill, and head towards the Churchillian Pub (*Page 62, bottom*) - where Widley Walk heads off to the left. Follow it down the side of Fort Widley, into the valley, and keep going as it twists and turns until you reach the T-junction with Purbrook Heath Road. Take a right here and follow this until you reach the tennis courts and the Rowan's Hospice (which is where the short-cut above brings you out). The section you are now walking along follows the route of the old Roman road which ran from Chichester to Southampton.

To the right of the gates to the hospice, take the woodland path until you reach the main roundabout (you could stay on the main road, but the path is the prettier option).

B At the roundabout, where there is a chippy and a café if you need refreshments, head straight across to Ladybridge Road, which you follow for about a mile (crossing another roundabout) until you reach the right-hand turning for Southdowns College, aptly named College Road. Head towards the college, where on the left is the entrance into Gundymoor Woods (*opposite bottom*). Take the yellow trail through the woods behind Southdown's College, past the fields (under which are the remains of a Roman villa), until you reach the bridge over the A3 (Scratchface Lane). Keep walking to the playing field then take the third right, Maylands Road. This brings you to a triangle with some trees in it, where you take the left-hand diagonal road (still Maylands Road), heading south-east, leading to a roundabout on Bedhampton Road. On the opposite side, to the left, is Brookside Road, which you want to head down until you reach a T-junction.

C We're going to take a small diversion here: at the T-junction head left along Bidbury Lane (towards the Bowls Club) and ahead is the church of St. Thomas. The oldest parts of the church date back to c1140, but in the grounds are two magnificent yew trees. The oldest of these is at least 600 years old (*right*), and there are some who put it between 700 to 900 years old. If we go back to the younger estimate of 600 years to 1421, this was the year King Henry VI was born, and there was only 16 years left to go of the One Hundred Years War. The oldest tree in Britain, which is also a yew, has a few more years on this one though with an age of somewhere between two and three thousand years old (the Fortingall Yew in Perthshire).

Once you have explored the church and churchyard, go back along Bidbury Lane and stay straight as it turns into Lower Road. This will meet the large Bedhampton roundabout (with the A3 flyover). Cross the roundabout by taking the north path towards the Rusty Cutter and then the west path towards Drayton, so you are now on the Havant Road. Walk along this until you reach Rectory Avenue (not Old Rectory Road).

Originally, there was a diversion on this walk to carry on straight ahead to St. Andrews Church, just ahead of you on the Havant Road. Up until Storm Eunice in 2022, there were two yew trees in the churchyard, one of which was dated at around 480 years old (*left, in 2021 before the storm*).

Though this church was heavily rebuilt in the 1870's, there are records indicating a church was here (or hereabouts) since the twelfth century, which would help tie in with the age of the yews. 480 years ago, in 1541, the Mary Rose was already 30 years old (and just 4 years away from sinking), and Henry VIII was on the throne of England. Seeing castles and fortifications of stone from that period is one thing, being able to see and touch something that has been alive through the centuries is always special, and losing these trees is rather sad. I've left the mention of this tree, though now gone, as it was often referred to as the oldest tree in the Portsmouth City Council jurisdiction.

Head up Rectory Avenue, turn right at the top taking you along Woodfield Avenue, then go up the hill until you reach Portsdown Hill Road.

For another shortcut, you can now head straight along the road back to the car park you started from, shaving half a mile from your route - it is worth heading up onto the top of the hill though as you get some of the best views of Farlington and the marshes from there.

D Cross the road at the waste management plant where a path on the left heads up into the shrubs. Follow this round past Farlington Redoubt, which now houses several companies, but unfortunately nothing remains of the redoubt as it was quarried out (with a lot of the chalk being used for the construction of the Eastern Road). This was originally the eastern end of the fortifications along Portsdown Hill that protected Portsea Island.

The path takes you north, turning left at the golf course (there should be a wooden gate blocking your way onto the golf course). Stay on this path past the horse paddocks, using the stiles to cross. When you get to a T-junction with a tarmac path, turn right and head north towards South Downs College. Passing the entrance to the golf club (on this side), there is a subway to cross under Crookhorn Lane (which turns back into College Road a bit further on). Cross, and head back up the hill towards Fort Purbrook. You will see more horse paddocks, with the path bending right between two of them. Follow this until you reach the junction, where you take the right-hand fork which takes you behind and around Fort Purbrook. On the far side you come to a branch in the path, with a decent view of Langstone Harbour in the middle (*above*). Take the right-hand fork towards the World War II lookout shelter (*left*), staying on this path between the houses and the golf course. Eventually it turns left back to Portsdown Hill Road and the car park where you started.

If you haven't stopped for a drink yet, then now is the perfect time to pop into the Churchillian (*below*) to recharge.

Benches: Top of Portsdown Hill

Picnic Areas: Top of Portsdown Hill

Pubs: The Churchillian, Rusty Cutter Beefeater

Public Toilets: None (Asda Havant is close to South Downs College)

Cafes: Mick's Monster Burgers, 1st Quay Fish & Chips,

Shops: The Village Bakery (Purbrook)

Birds of the Hampshire Coast

Black-headed Gull

Barnacle Goose

Avocet

Curlew

Cormorant

Grey Heron

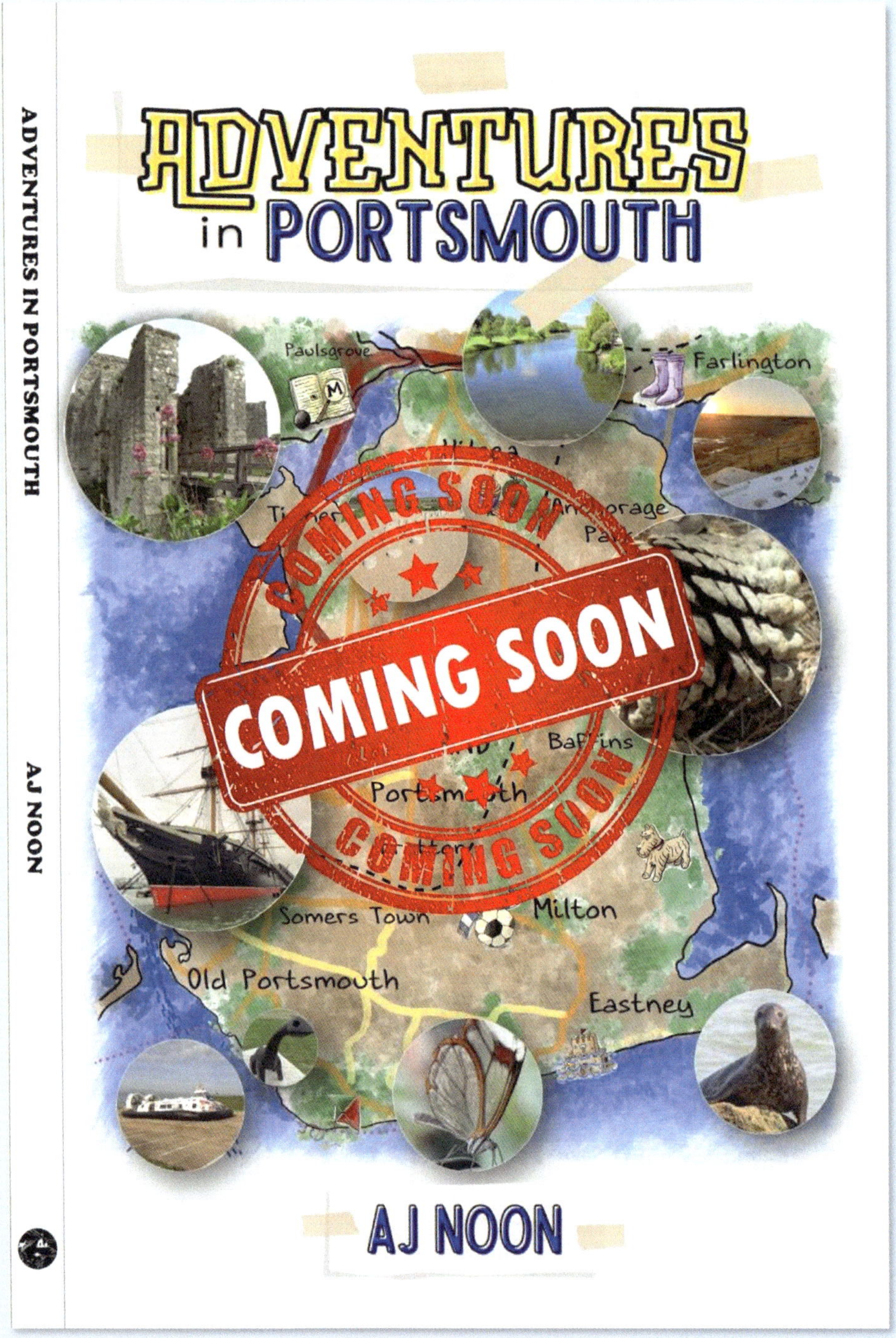
ADVENTURES IN PORTSMOUTH
AJ NOON
ADVENTURES
in PORTSMOUTH
Paulsgrove
Farlington
Baffins
Somers Town
Milton
Old Portsmouth
Eastney
COMING SOON
AJ NOON

CHARLES II. AND THE DUCHESS OF PORTSMOUTH.

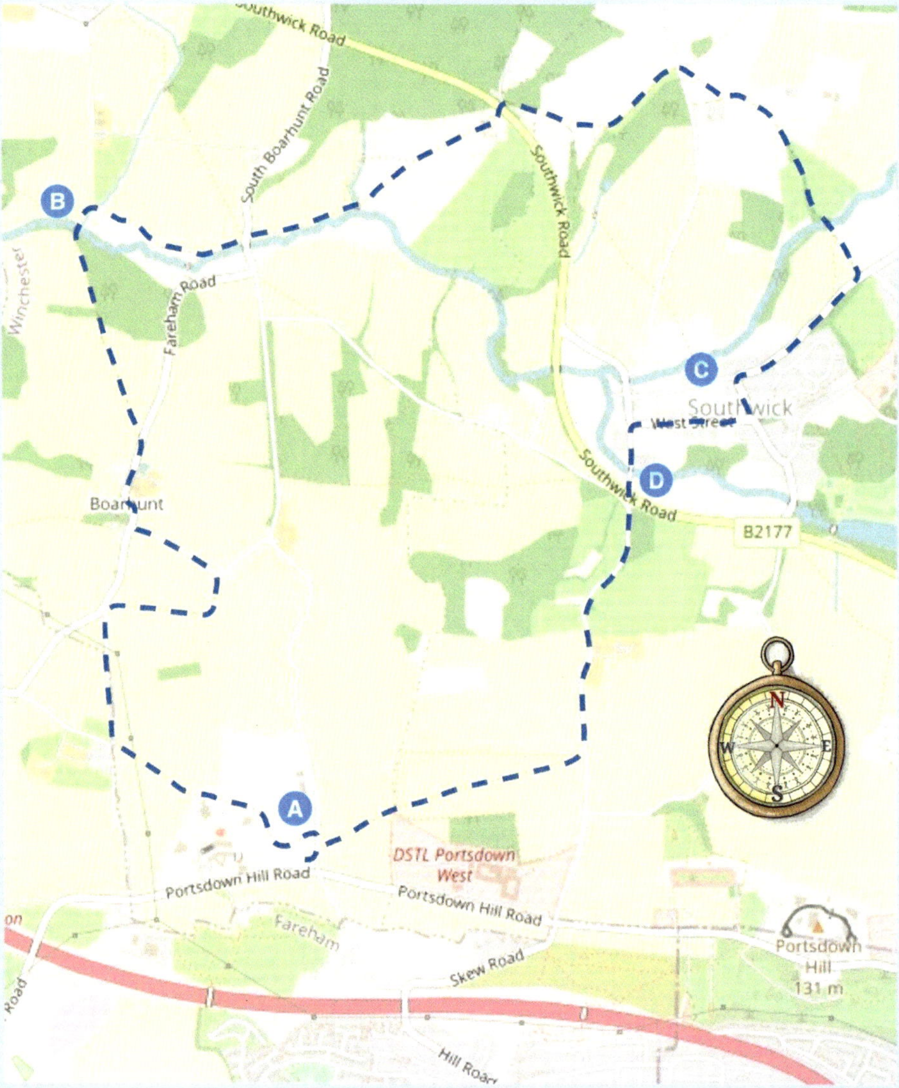
Southwick Road
South Boarhunt Road
Southwick Road
B
A
C
D
Winchester
Fareham Road
Southwick
West Street
Southwick Road
B2177
Boarhunt
N
W
E
S
DSTL Portsdown West
Portsdown Hill Road
Portsdown Hill Road
Fareham
Skew Road
Portsdown Hill
131 m
Hill Road

N4. Trafalgar to D-Day

6.25 Miles | 2 Hours | 410 Ft Ascent

Track, grass, and some road

Parking: Fort Nelson, PO17 6AN (Pay, 10:00-16:00)
Bus: Golden Lion (Southwick), 38
Nearest Train Station: Portchester (1.25 Miles)

This walk takes you from the top of Portsdown Hill, down to Southwick, and back. It's a great introductory walk for exploring some of the paths on the 'other side' of the hill and gives you a mix of terrains to walk on. If you are lucky, you may see deer, buzzards, and red kites on this walk.

There are two sections where you have to walk on the road, though these are quite quiet, and one small section where it can get muddy.

A Starting at the Nelson Monument by Fort Nelson, walk left down Monument Lane a short way until you see a gate and signpost on your left. Go through the gate and follow the path around the reservoir, behind Fort Nelson, then across the fields until it reaches the road.

Fort Nelson is one of *'Palmerston's Follies'*, fortifications ordered by the then Prime Minister Lord Palmerston, and nicknamed follies as the threat of invasion from France had passed by the time they were completed in 1867. There were 4 forts in the Solent and 23 fortifications on and surrounding Portsmouth, which were designed to protect not only Portsea Island from attack by sea, but also from an invasion force that may be landed further up the coast who could then attack the dockyard from behind.

Fort Nelson opened as a museum (part of the Royal Armouries collection) in 1994 and is free to visit. In summer they usually fire one of their guns every day at noon, and you can sit outside with drinks from their café, so it is well worth a visit. The Nelson Monument, which gave the fort its' name, was completed in 1808 and at 120 feet tall is used as a navigation landmark for shipping. It required a rebuild in 1899 and, oddly, its position means it falls under Winchester City Council, not Portsmouth.

At the road, turn right and follow it until it reaches the junction with Boarhunt Road. This corner can be quite dangerous as there is no path to avoid the traffic, so take the track cutting across the field to your right just before the junction. Cross the field until halfway, where a track joins it from the left. Turn onto the track, keeping to the left fork when it splits, and follow it back to the road.

Now you will turn right, passing the church car park and a series of large brick farm buildings. After the farm with the large pond on your right, go through the farm gate and track on the left (highlighted by a footpath signpost). Head along the track to the trees and take your time as you walk for this area is great for deer-spotting, especially early in the morning. You may also spot yellowhammers and brown hares (*opposite*).

B You reach a gap in the trees, taking you through to the next field. Keep along the right edge until a small concrete bridge (*right*) crossing the river Wallington (which comes out in Fareham Creek) in the corner. Cross the bridge, then follow the path round to the right, where it meets a gate. Go through the gate and cross the field (keeping the trees and shrubs in the middle immediately to your left). At the far end, the path curves to your left

and then reaches a gate to the road. Cross here, picking up the path on the other side, before crossing another field. Stay to the right of the mound to the far side, where it then follows the field boundary to the right, before going through another gate where you reach the farmers track. Follow this through the dairy farm (making sure to keep the gates closed behind you).

Cross the road after the farm, taking the track to the right and go through another gate. Follow this for a short way until you come out of the trees, where there is a gate on your left crossing the field. Pairs of posts across the field mark the path for you to take. At the far side, cross the road (Common Lane), and into another field. The path now goes diagonally across the field to your right (you can walk round the edge if it is easier), where it reaches a farm track. A few feet to your left should be a track junction and heading diagonally between these is a grass path with hedges on each side. Head down this track and follow it to the main road leading into Southwick. You pass one small but muddy section and another bridge over the river Wallington before reaching the road.

C At the main road, turn right and head into Southwick, turning into the High Street on your left when you reach it. There are a couple of great pubs and a tearoom in Wallington, so now is a good time to stop for refreshments. One thing to note with Southwick is the doors of the houses are all painted the same (*right*). The village is owned and run by the Southwick Estate, and one of the conditions of the tenancy agreement is that the doors must be red.

Southwick House, which is down Priory Road on the left after the church, was a major planning centre for Operation Overlord (D-Day) during World War II. It was built in 1800, and in 1943 became the advance command post for the invasion operations. General Eisenhower, Admiral Ramsay, and General Montgomery were all based there for the undertaking. It is now home to the Defence School of Policing and Guarding and can only be visited by appointment, however they have regular open days when groups can visit. The village hosts the *'Southwick Revival'* every June which commemorates D-Day and raises funds for several charities. Vintage vehicles, costumes, music and more all feature, making it a grand day out.

Opposite the church is West Street (look for the red phone box) which you need to go down until you reach a T-junction. Take the left branch, Fareham Road, heading back towards Portsdown Hill.

D Follow this path, using the stiles to cross the field (I've yet to see the bull that lives there, but please be careful), and you come to a road junction of the B2177 and Ham Road. Cross over, then take the left road (Portchester Lane) and follow this uphill.

After two large farms on your left, is a footpath sign on the right pointing out across the fields and back to Nelson's Monument. Walk across the fields (there is an easier path further up on your right just after Crooked Walk Lane which you may prefer) until you get back to the monument.

Benches: Top of Portsdown Hill, Southwick

Picnic Areas: Top of Portsdown Hill

Pubs: The Red Lion, The Golden Lion

Public Toilets: None

Cafes: Fort Nelson

Shops: Southwick Village Store

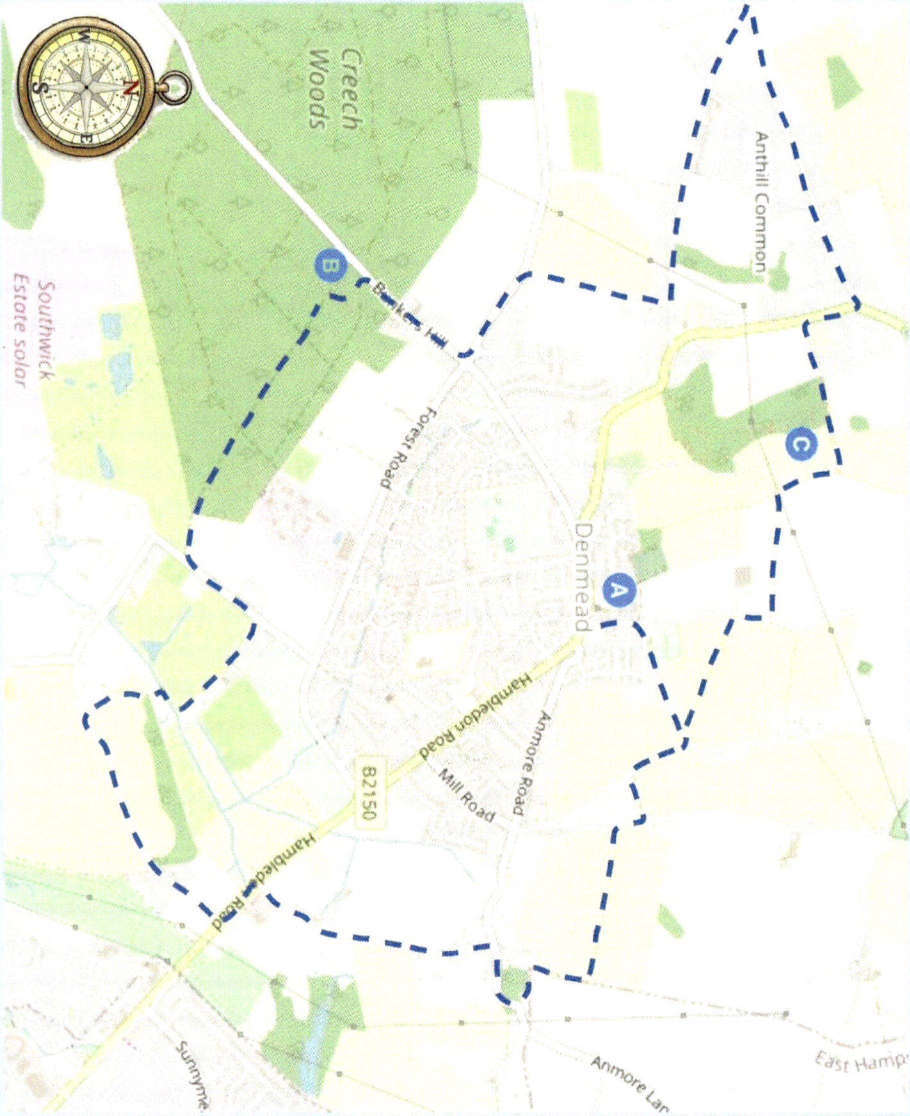

Creech Woods
Southwick Estate solar
Anthill Common
Bunkers Hill
Forest Road
Denmead
Hambledon Road
B2150
Mill Road
Anmore Road
Anmore Lar
East Hamp
Sunnyme
A
B
C
N
S
E
W

N5. Denmead Millennium Trail

7.5 Miles | 2 Hours 30 Mins | 12 Ft Ascent

All pavement

Parking: Kidmore Lane Car Park, PO7 6JZ (free), Creech Wood, PO7 6UB (Free)

Bus: Denmead Green, D1, D2, 652, 654 (all from Waterlooville)

This walk has large sections along country lanes, so is not ideal for taking young children or dogs, however if you do have either then a separate visit to Creech Wood (PO7 6UB) is recommended, especially now they have the signage up for the remains of the camps that were built for the troops assembling for Operation Overlord.

A This route goes anti-clockwise, but at the start it feels like you are going clockwise. There are some markers along the route, but not all the way around, '*Millennium Trail*'.

Leave the car park and head up Kidmore Lane, turning right onto Tanners Lane at the Scout hut. A few hundred yards down the road (before Whitehorse Lane) there is a stile on the left (*main picture*). Cross into the field and continue towards the oak tree on your left, keeping left of the large depression and aiming for the farm buildings in the distance. Keep on past the tree until you reach the road (Kidmore Lane again), where you turn right. A short way on your left, go through the gate by the farm and follow the hedge-line. The track turns left along the side of the field following the electric fence. Where it crosses the farm track you will need to unhook (and re-hook) the electric wires - please be careful.

Carry on to the end of the field, cross the stile, then follow the track right. When you cross into the next field, turn left and head up to the trees, following the hedgerow - this area is a great place to spot deer (*opposite*). The path goes through the trees and straight on to Hambledon Road (ignore the side turnings), and when you reach the road head right for a few hundred yards until you reach Uplands Road. Take this road (carefully as there is no pavement) to the crossroads with the old-fashioned signpost (about half-a-mile along).

At the crossroads, turn left into School Lane and follow this to Inhams Lane on your right (passing the Fox & Hounds pub, which is a decent place to stop for refreshments). Head down Inhams Lane, turn left at the end onto Forest Road and keep on to the double roundabout. Go right up Bunkers Hill until you reach Creech Wood - when the pavement ends on the left take the forest path that runs parallel to the road and into the carpark.

B Creech Wood was one of the staging posts for Operation Overlord in World War II, and there are the remains of many buildings and facilities in the forest. Project 71, a veteran's charity, have helped supply information boards explaining the site and how it was used (*above*). There is one picnic bench here, and the woods are a great place to explore at any time.

Go through the car park until you reach a single signpost on a wide track (*left*), take a left and stay on this track until it turns into a bridleway and then Furzeley Road. Take the next left, and after the entrance to the golf club is a right (signposted to the

'Driving Range') which you need to head down. When you reach the brick building there is a small path to the right of it leading to a wooden bridge crossing the river. Cross, and you should now be standing at the edge of the golf course. The footpath cuts diagonally across the course to your left to a stile you should be able to make out in the treeline, which you need to head for - please be careful crossing the course. After the stile, the track crosses a field then reaches Closewood Lane, which you follow to the junction with Hambledon Road,

Here, turn left, then right down Soake Road. Again, there is no path here and it is quite twisty, so pay extra attention to the traffic. After the Aquatics Centre you reach the junction with Anmore Lane, where you turn right. Follow this round the bend until you reach a yellow gravel path on the left (on the opposite side of the road is a bridleway heading into the trees). The gravel path, though it looks like a private drive, is the route to take, and it goes between a house and a garage before running alongside a very large pit.

C The path curves to the right then comes out on an open field. This is where you need to be a bit careful as the route is not obvious. You should see the path straight in front of you heading along the hedgerow that runs most of the way between the two fields. Walk to the hedgerow and keep on the right-hand side of it. Shortly after passing the hedge there is another path to your left. Take this (so you are walking away from the pylons) and follow it across to Edneys Lane.

Here, turn right, and when you reach the farm track marked *'Merrits Farms Ctts'* (*above*) take this left turn. At the end of this track, turn right down White Hart Lane, and at the next junction turn left onto Tanner's Lane. At the end of the road is the Scout hut again so turn left to get back to the car park.

If you need refreshments, the Forest of Bere pub is just to the west of the car park on the main road, or there are shops along to the right after the car park.

Benches: Creech Wood

Picnic Areas: Creech Wood

Pubs: The Forest of Bere, the White Hart, the Harvest Home, the Fox & Hounds

Public Toilets: at the starting point

Cafes: 10 min walk from starting point, Barnard's Restaurant

Shops: Co-op, newsagent, bakery, chemist, in Denmead

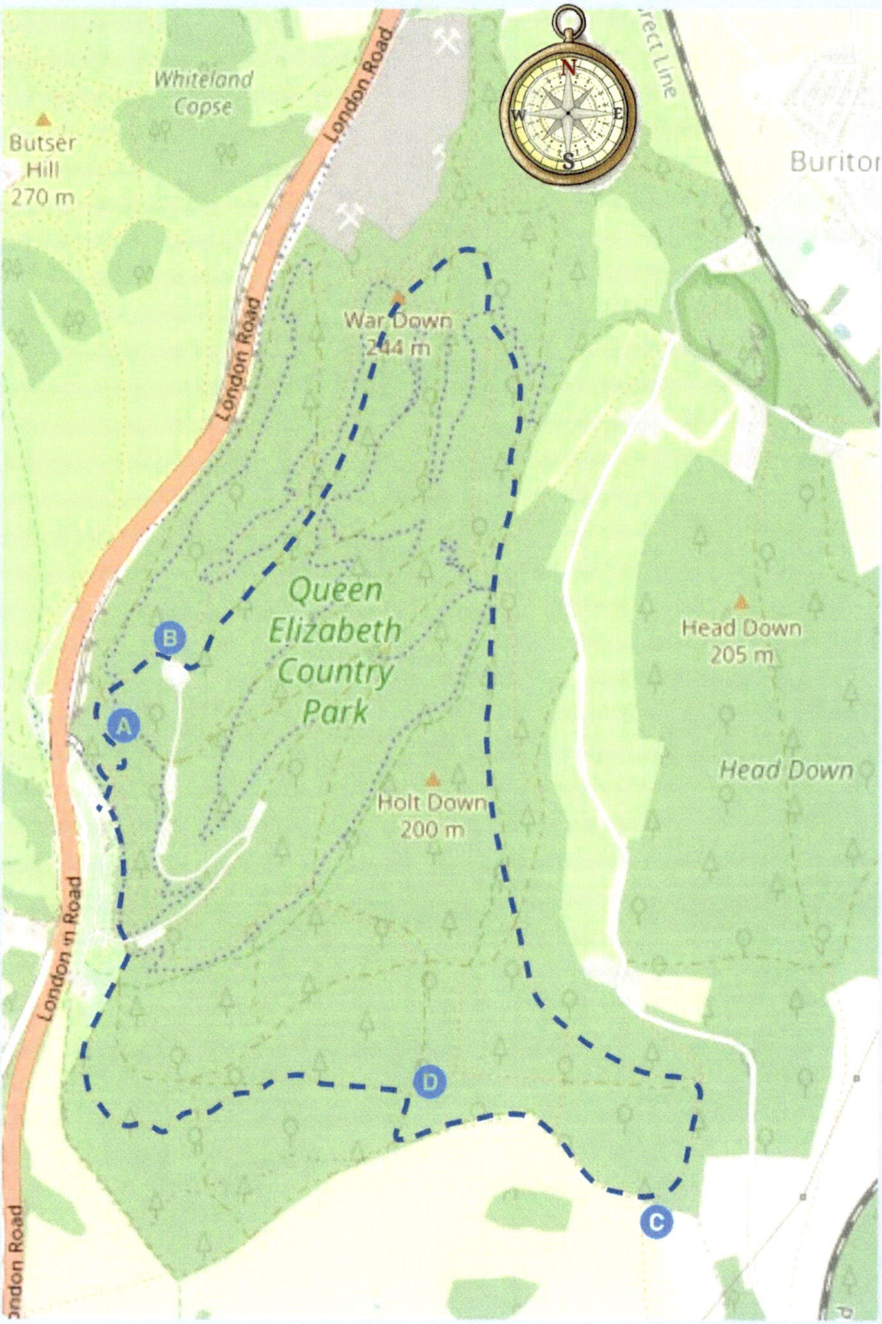
Whiteland Copse
Butser Hill 270 m
London Road
Buritor
War Down 244 m
London Road
Queen Elizabeth Country Park
B
A
Head Down 205 m
Head Down
Holt Down 200 m
London Road
D
C
London Road

N6. Queen Elizabeth Country Park

5 Miles | 2 Hours 0 Mins | 650 Ft Ascent

Gravel and Woodland Trails

Parking: QE Country Park, PO8 0QE (£4.50 for 4 hours Oct-Mar, £7 for 4 hours Apr-Sep)

Bus: 37 & 637 (Havant to Petersfield)

Train: Havant (10 Miles)

There are several walking routes already marked out in the park, including the Short Woodland Trail (1.9 miles, marked by green dashes), the Downland Trail (1.7 miles, marked by a solid red line), and the Long Woodland Trail (5 miles, marked by purple dashes on the map and purple footprints on the trail - *below*). In the Visitor Centre by the main car park you can purchase a map with these trails marked out, as well as the picnic areas and other facilities. Alternatively, you can just follow the signs that mark out the trails in the park.

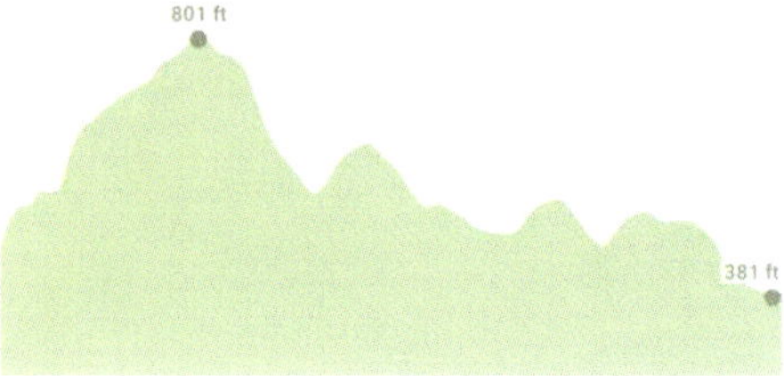

Queen Elizabeth Country Park is a great place for exercising the dog, though there are some areas where they need to be kept on their lead. They have recently introduced a dog-wash station at the Visitor Centre, so if you have a pooch who likes to get mucky you can give them a clean before putting them back in your car.

For this walk, I've picked the pre-marked 5-mile Woodland Trail, which gives you a good introduction to the area, including the types of trails available, the BBQ areas, the play areas, and even the exercise areas if you want to add more of a workout to your walk.

*NB: If you have the time and the energy, you can also add walk **N6a** – Butser Hill onto this walk as they both start and end at the main car park.*

Just in front of the Visitor Centre is a path on the left that leads up into the woods – head this way and follow the purple trail signs for the next 5 miles. There are a couple of places where the signs can be overgrown or are not obvious, which I have highlighted on the map.

A The first one is when you come to a broad path that crosses yours, in this instance you keep heading up (the signpost for it is in the undergrowth on the other side of the path).

B When you get to Juniper car park at the top, keep to the left-hand side until you reach a broad gravel track heading off to your left. This is the main track to follow, though watch out for cars if you are there at peak summertime. In this section are picnic and BBQ areas (*above middle*), play areas (*above*), toilets, a café, and exercise fixtures.

Follow this track as it loops around the top of the hill, until you share a section with the Staunton Way.

C When the path reaches the fields at the southernmost section, it curves round to your right, through the forest, and then back to the Visitor Centre.

D **Note, there can be foresters working in the park, and there may be signed diversions.**

Benches: Plenty

Picnic Areas: Plenty + specific BBQ Areas

Public Toilets: Visitor Centre, Juniper car park

Cafes: Visitor Centre, Juniper car park

Pubs: The Hampshire Hog, 10 min walk South from the main car park

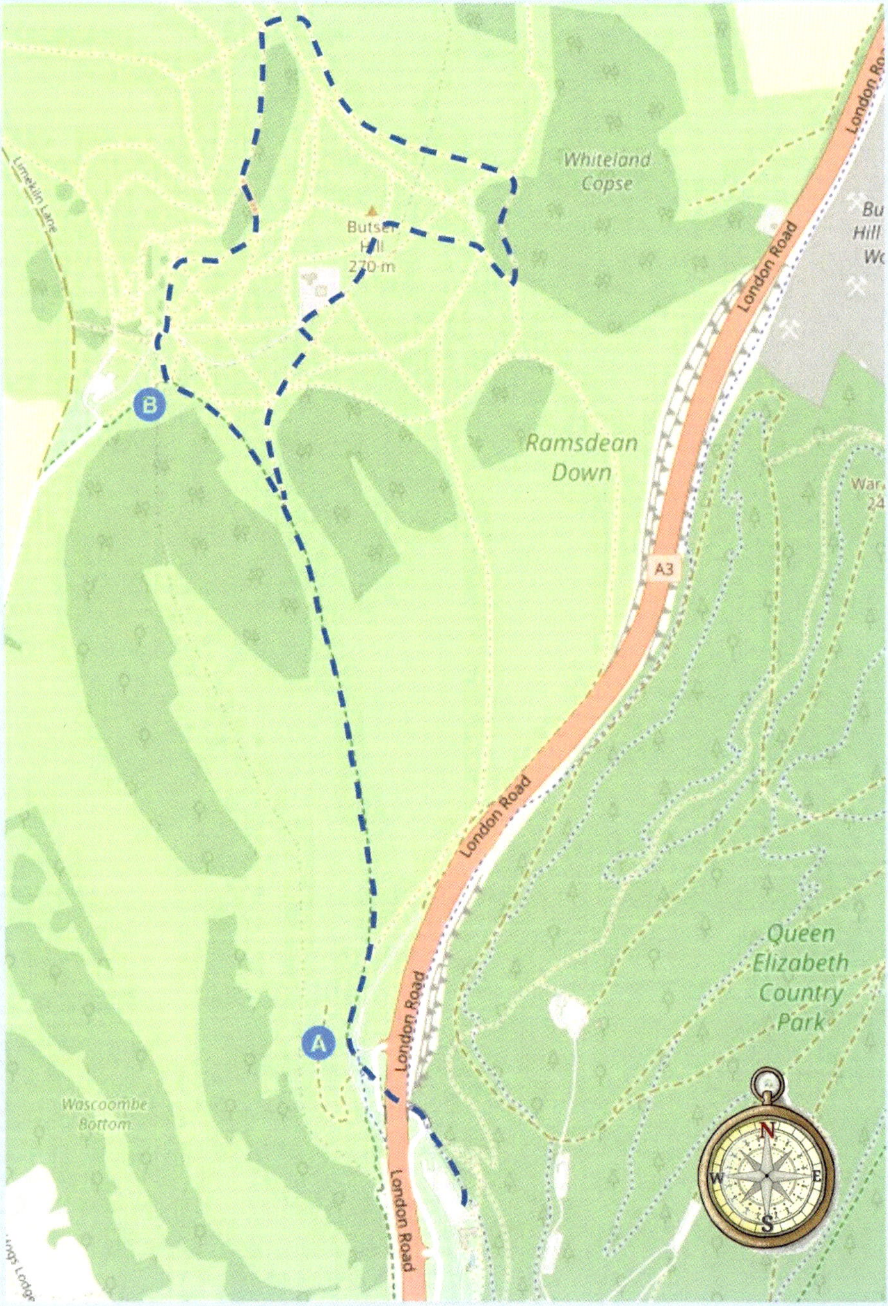
Whiteland Copse
Butser Hill
270 m
Limekiln Lane
Ramsdean Down
A3
London Road
Queen Elizabeth Country Park
Wascoombe Bottom
N
E
S
W

N6a. Butser Hill

3.75 Miles 1 Hours 30 Mins 675 Ft Ascent

Gravel and Grassland Trails

Parking: QE Country Park, PO8 0QE (£4.50 for 4 hours Oct-Mar, £7 for 4 hours Apr-Sep)

Bus: 37 & 637 (Havant to Petersfield),

Train: Havant (10 Miles)

Whilst you are at Queen Elizabeth Country Park, there is a nice short walk you can add on to any of the main ones (see **N6**), which is a quick jaunt up to the top of Butser Hill and back. Butser, with the top at 885 feet (270 metres) above sea-level, is the second highest hill in Hampshire (the highest being Pilot Hill near Highclere Castle). Aside from the views, there is an excellent area at the top set aside for kite-flying,

From the main car park, head away from the visitor centre towards the barriers where there is a path on the right-hand side of the road. Stay on the low path under the A3 (the high one takes you up to the A3 and the bus stops) until you come to the gated track on your left which leads to the barbeque areas.

Go through the gate and the path will come to a small crossroads (*left*).

A The path you want is the middle one, carrying slightly to the right. It dips down through the trees until you come out looking at Butser Hill (*main picture*).

This path will now lead you up the hill, and through a gate about two-thirds of the way up. After the gate, there is a split in the grass paths, and you want to take the left one (marked *South Downs Way*). If you haven't yet, stop and look behind you - if it is a clear day you should be able to see the Isle of Wight and the Spinnaker Tower.

B Head to the next gate, then once through go immediately to your right up the chalk path with hedges on each side. This leads you to the café (*right*), where there are picnic benches and toilets. NB: the café only tends to be open in the busy periods such as school holidays and half-terms. Once you have refreshed yourself, go through the metal gate opposite the café and you are now going to follow the red trail around the top of Butser Hill and back to where the path forked. By the gate is a map of the area with the red trail marked out - it looks like a giant splat on the top of Butser.

The trail is nicely marked, so stick with the signposts as it goes around the hill, giving you good views in all directions. Just after you come back past the communications tower you re-join the path where you came up the hill – take this back down to the car park.

The A3, which separates Butser Hill and QE Country Park, was the main route to London, and required regular maintenance. Because of the costs involved it became a turnpike (a toll road) in 1711, and in 1770 the coach journey from London to Portsmouth would take 16 hours on the quickest coaches. The area further north, between Petersfield and Hindhead, became rife with highwaymen and bandits. One of the most notorious of them, James Allen, was eventually shot dead near Midhurst in 1807.

Benches: Butser Kiosk

Picnic Areas: Specific BBQ Areas

Public Toilets: Visitor Centre, Butser Kiosk

Cafes: Butser Kiosk, Visitor Centre

Pubs: The Hampshire Hog, 10 min walk

East of Portsea Island

To the east of Portsea Island lie two more islands, Hayling and Thorney. In the Domesday Book of 1086, Hayling Island had 83 households recorded and Thorney Island had 43 households, making them both far more populous than Portsea Island. Hayling is noted as having salt pans for salt production and was a base for shell fishing and farming. The remains of an Iron Age shrine, which had a Roman temple built over the top of it, have been discovered on Hayling, though there are no other visible traces left.

Hayling has a chequered history, with William I giving ownership of most of the land to the abbey of Jumièges, near Le Havre. Later English kings decided they weren't happy with the French owning English land so took it back, with Henry VIII eventually granting jurisdiction to the Holy Trinity College of Arundel in 1541.

Seaside spa towns in the UK started booming at the start of the 1700's and, being no slouch, Hayling Island tried to turn themselves into a seaside resort in the early 1820's, with the railway arriving in 1867. Okay, so that is a little disingenuous, in 1801 there was a population of less than 600 on the island, hardly ideal for starting a spa town, and a bridge across Sweare Deep (the name of the channel) wasn't built until 1824. This bridge was a toll bridge, and though the current bridge was opened in 1956 it wasn't until 1960 that tolls were abolished.

The last trains ran to Hayling Island in 1963, and it is the old railway track that makes the best walking on the island, asides from the beach. The population has also grown over the years, with nearly 17,000 people now living there.

Thorney Island juts into Chichester Harbour, but most of it is dedicated to a military base, which can make walking round it awkward at times. There are two gates with buzzers for you to be let through to follow the coastal path, but it is not unknown for the calls to be unanswered, or access denied if there are military exercises running.

In 1936, the Air Ministry purchased Thorney Island, leaving them with the small problem of what to do with the 300 inhabitants who had long been settled there.

Everyone was moved inland, leaving only the church (*above*) and churchyard behind, and the RAF base opened in 1938. In the run-up to D-Day, Typhoon squadrons flew from here to take out German early-warning and radar stations monitoring the English Channel, with over 4,000 personnel based here.

In 1984, the Army, specifically the 26th Field Regiment Royal Artillery, took over the base and have run it since. The airfield is still used, and you can frequently see light aircraft taking off and landing.

Finally, we have the estates of Staunton and Stansted (*left*), both of which have some great walking routes. Stansted, in Spring, has great swathes of bluebells and foxgloves.

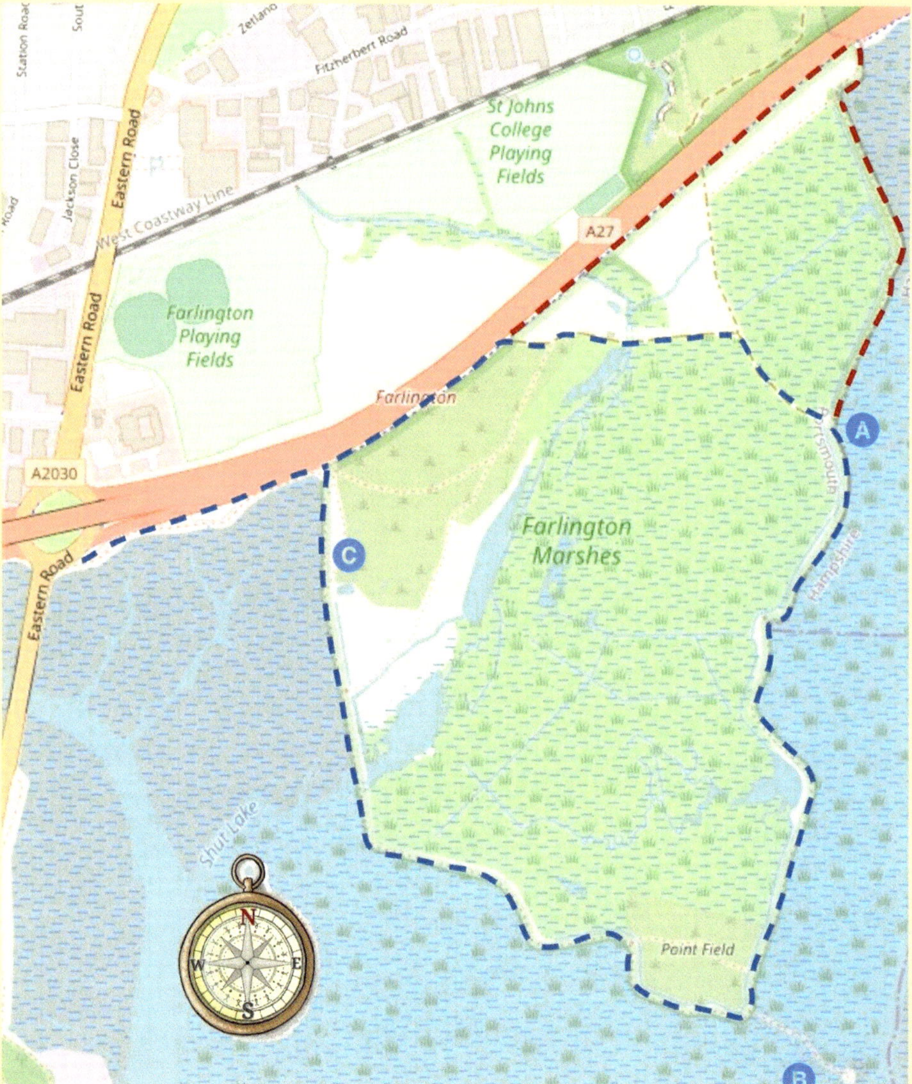
St Johns College Playing Fields
Farlington Playing Fields
Farlington Marshes
Eastern Road
West Coastway Line
Jackson Close
Station Road
Fitzherbert Road
A27
A2030
Farlington
Shut Lake
Point Field
Portsmouth
Hampshire
A
B
C
N
E
S
W

E1. Farlington Marshes

This is a superb walk for the nature lover, with Farlington Marshes being home to many species of birds, and in Winter it provides an important food source for migratory birds. This ensures that if you visit over the course of a year, you will see different species each time.

3/3.5 Miles | 1 Hr 15 Mins | 0 Ft Ascent

Gravel and potentially Muddy Tracks

Parking: Farlington Marshes (Free), PO6 1SR

Bus: Walton Road, 21, 621

Nearest Train Station: Cosham (3 Miles)

There are two main routes for Farlington Marshes, one a 3-mile loop from the entrance, the other is 3.5-miles.

This walk is simple: from the car park, follow the coastal path anti-clockwise in a loop until you get back to the car park.

A The only decision you have to make is at the two-mile point, where you can choose to head towards the brick visitor centre by taking the left-hand path or continuing along the coast. Sticking to the coastal path will add half a mile to your total distance, but this section gets very muddy in winter/wet weather, so you may need to exercise caution.

Whichever path you take, the final section is shared with cyclists, so please be alert at this point as not everyone uses a bell to warn pedestrians as they approach.

B The marshes were first reclaimed from the sea in 1771, when they were used for oyster fishing and hunting wildfowl, though oysters have been taken from the harbour since Roman times. There used to be a house (built in 1819) out in the harbour itself, and at low tide you can see remains of its base. The house shows up in the 1841 census, where it is named '*New Milton*', but it fell into disuse in the 20th Century.

The marshes are a *Hampshire and Isle of Wight Wildlife Trust* reserve, and they have provided information boards (*above*) around the walk to help you identify the many bird species you should see. Just by the main entry, and in the information building, there are boards (*right*) that are updated with the birds that have been seen recently. There are usually many ornithologists around who will gladly tell you what you can see, and included in the list are: avocets, dunlins, flycatchers, reed and sedge warblers, marsh harriers, and lapwings. If you take a walk at dusk, you have a good chance of spotting an owl or two as well.

There are three small car parks along the access road, and by the last one is a gate that takes you into the reserve. Head right at the noticeboard and up onto the sea wall for just over 2 miles until you come to a fork in the path. Taking the right-hand option, staying with the seawall, takes you along the potentially muddy route which adds half a mile to your walk distance (3.5 miles in total). Taking the left fork, which heads inland towards the information building, gives you a total walk distance of 3 miles.

C During the Second World War, the marshes were used as a '*starfish*' site. Fires were lit to simulate burning buildings in the hope it would attract the Luftwaffe to bomb this area rather than the buildings on Portsea Island itself. The two brick bunkers you will see on your walk (*above*) were for the servicemen who ran these sites. There are still three large craters that can be made out in the marshes from this bombing.

Benches: Frequent

Picnic Areas: None

Pubs: None

Public Toilets: None

Cafes: None

Shops: Shell Garage 5 mins walk from the car park

A train on the Hayling Billy Line - note it has both passenger and cargo carriages

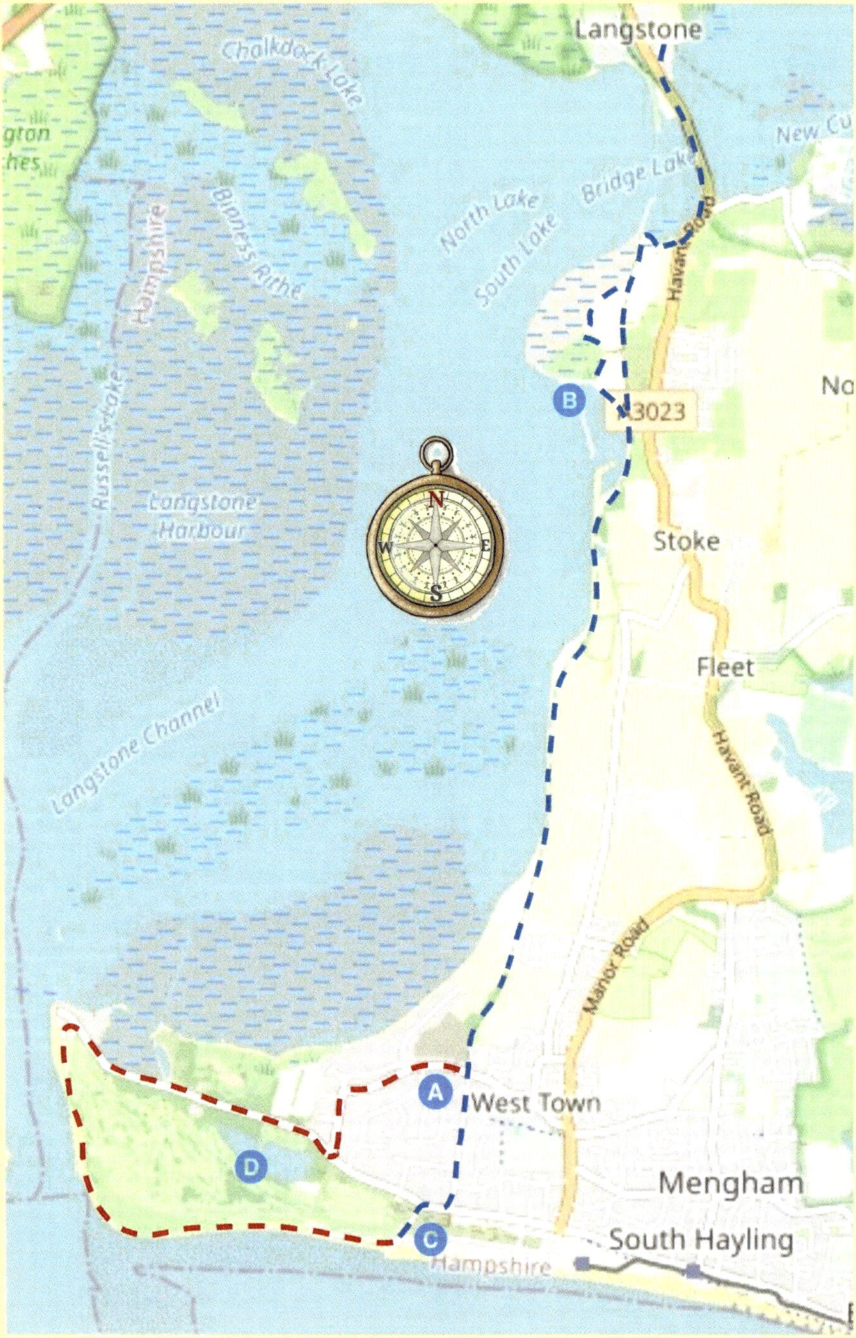

Langstone
Chalkdock Lake
New Cu
Bridge Lake
North Lake
South Lake
Hampshire
Bipness Rithe
Havant Road
Russell's Lake
B
A3023
No
Langstone Harbour
N
W
E
S
Stoke
Fleet
Langstone Channel
Havant Road
Manor Road
A
West Town
D
Mengham
C
South Hayling
Hampshire

E2. Hayling Billy Trail

7 or 11 Miles | 2.5 or 4 Hours | 46 Ft Ascent

Track, Beach, and Pavement

Parking: Top end: Hayling Billy Line Car Park, PO11 0LW (free)*
Bottom end: West Beach Car Park, PO11 0AS (5 Hours £8)
Bus: West Beach, 30 and 31 from Havant
Nearest Train Station: Havant (2 Miles)

This walk has two options, a slightly shorter one at 7 miles, and a longer one at 11 miles. They take you from the beach at Hayling Island, up to the top of the Hayling Billy Trail and the Ship Inn, and then back down the trail. If you want the longer option, you can then go round Gunnery Point (where the Hayling Island to Eastney ferry lands) and back to the starting point at West Beach.

Like many routes that run along old train tracks, parts of this are tree-lined giving you decent shade on hot days.

Facing away from the beach at West Beach car park, take the inland road to the right of John's Café (with public toilets just behind it). When it meets the main road (called Sea Front) follow the signs to the right which say Havant, then take Staunton Avenue on your left, with signs pointing to '*Station Theatre*'. When you reach it, the theatre was originally the goods shed for the trains that ran into Hayling station, which was a bit further up to the left of this building. As a goods shed, it was completed in 1901, but came up for sale in 1992. After fund-raising campaigns, and a lot of hard work, the first theatrical performance (Tom Stoppard's *Travesties*) took place on July 27th, 1996.

A To the left of the theatre is a path that is the bottom end of the Hayling Billy Trail. You now have a straight 3 mile walk up to the top end of the trail, the Haying Billy Line Car Park. When you get to the Billy Trail car park - about two-thirds of the way - stay on the main trail – we will go past the Oyster Beds (signposted to the left) on the way back.

There are plenty of information boards along the route, explaining both the importance of the area as a wildlife haven and the remains of the World War II defences (*left*).

Carry on past the car park and along the bridge over the sea channel called '*Sweare Deep*' until get you to the Ship Inn on the right-hand side. Another pub, the Royal Oak, is slightly further along, so there are a couple of options for refreshments and/or a meal. When you are refreshed, head back down to the Trail. Just after the small Hayling Billy Car Park, where the trail starts, there is a turning on your right marked '*Oyster Beds*'. Take this path and follow it round.

B Oysters were farmed here from the early 19th Century, though by the 1970's had fallen out of use. The area was restored in 1996 and is now an important breeding area for seabirds. The RSPB are always looking for volunteers to help monitor and protect the area and you should see signs for how to volunteer (*right, an Avocet*).

Follow this trail past the beds until you re-join the main Hayling Billy trail and return to the Station Theatre.

C If you are doing the shorter 7-mile option, head down Staunton Avenue ahead of you and back across the dunes to the car park where you started.

For the 11-mile option turn right onto Sinah Lane and follow it until you get to a fork in the road. To reduce the amount of road walking you need to do, take the left-hand fork (Park Road) until it re-joins Sinah Lane where you turn left. There is no pavement on this section so please take care.

At the end of Sinah Lane, turn right onto Ferry Road, passing the Sinah Warren holiday camp. The camp was originally a site run by monks from the 15th Century, and during World War II it became a factory farm to help provide food. In 1958 Warner's opened the site as a holiday camp.

D On your left are the remains of a heavy anti-aircraft battery built in 1940. There is not much left of the buildings, but there are information boards explaining the layout and role of the area if you wish to make a small diversion to explore here. It was initially manned by Royal Artillery Gunners of 219 battery, then by the 368th and 16th units.

At the end of Ferry Road is another car park, the Ferryboat Inn – which has great views - and it is also where the ferry between Eastney and Hayling docks. Tickets for the ferry are £3 per person (one-way) and it runs between 8 am and 8 pm. If you are looking to start your walk here, then Bus 25 from the Hard in Portsmouth stops at the ferry terminal on the Eastney side.

When you reach the car park, if you don't want the ferry or the Inn, bear left where is a small café. The path then takes you onto the beach, which follows around Gunner Point (as this area is called) and back to West Beach car park. This area played an important role during World War II as it was heavily used in the training of troops in preparation for D-Day.

As you go round the Point, on the opposite side of the channel (Eastney) you will see the structures of Fort Cumberland (*above*). The first recorded fortification there is an earthwork battery in 1714, with a substantial fort built there from 1747. In 1785 reconstruction of the site started, enlarging the defences and using stone for all of the works. It was still an active site for the Royal Marines up until the 1970's and is now an English Heritage Centre for Archaeology and home to the Nautical Archaeology Society. Open Days and tours are available of the facilities, but these must be pre-booked in advance.

Visit www.heritageopendays.org.uk for details on these events.

Benches: Few

Picnic Areas: The Beach

Pubs: The Ship Inn, The Royal Oak, The Ferryboat Inn

Public Toilets: West Beach

Cafes: Gunner Point

Shops: None

Emsworth
Hermitage
Southbourne
A259 Main Road
Southbourne
Southbourne
Inlands Road
Thorney Road
Thorney Road
A
B
C
D
Hampshire
Emsworth Channel
West Sussex
Chichester
Prinsted Channel
Nutbourne Channel
Thorney Channel
Baker Barracks
Thorney Island
N
S
E
W

E3. Thorney Island

9 Miles | 3 Hours 30 Mins | 49 Ft Ascent

Pavement, Track, Shingle, Sand

Parking: South Street Car Park (Pay, 4 Hours £3.40), PO10 7EG

Bus: Hermitage Bridge (700, from The Hard)

Nearest Train Station: Emsworth (.40 Miles)

As well as its military history, Thorney Island is a stunning place for wildlife (*marsh harrier, main picture*). Access to the southern area is controlled by two security gates, where you may need to provide contact information before being allowed through. Once inside the MOD area, you must stay to the coastal path, do not stray from it (there are patrols and cameras monitoring the sensitive areas).

Before you set out for this walk, please check the tide times for the area as at the highest tides (or in rough weather) the beach and the section by St. Nicholas Church can be difficult to pass.

Starting from the South Street Car Park, head north up South Street to the junction with High Street and turn right. The road curves round to the left, becoming Queen Street - do not take the right-hand fork down King Street. Just after the Lord Raglan pub on the right is a signpost for the path taking you past, and then, under some new build houses. You come out onto a path with the old mill pond on one side and a small marina on the other (*above*). The track takes you past the weir and to Slipper Road, where you turn right (it is marked Private but is a public right-of-way) and go through the marina. Please take care in this area as it is a working yard and there can be heavy machinery moving boats around.

A At the end of the yard, turn right, and when you get to the bench (*left*), turn left and you are now on the coastal path which will take you around Thorney Island to Prinsted Beach. Keep an eye out for harbour seals in warm weather as they are known to sun themselves on the banks (*opposite, bottom*).

B A short way along the path you come to the first security gate – press the buzzer and they should let you through (you may have to wait a few minutes if they are on a coffee break). About two miles after the gate, is a small car park by the beach; do not take the road, stay on the coastal path. After the car park you come to a deviation in the path, the right-hand fork takes you to the beach (there is a warning sign here about nesting birds) but you want to take the left path through the sandy dunes. It is only a short, sandy stretch before you come to a gravel/tarmac track. Follow this as it curves around the island and past the east end of the runway (*below*).

The path takes you behind the sailing centre **C** then along past the church (where you need to be careful at high tide).

The church was established around 1178 (Norman) with 13th and 15th Century extensions and modifications. Services

H.M. THE KING INSPECTING AIRCRAFT, THORNEY ISLAND

are still held here and there is a dedicated area of the graveyard for service personnel.

Back on the coastal path, go through the second security gate, then when you reach a junction take the right path, staying with the coast.

As already mentioned, the area is a key reserve for birds, with herons, ibis, harriers, oystercatchers, plovers, cormorants, black-headed gulls (*juvenile, left*), and even the occasional migratory osprey passing through.

D You will reach Thornham Marina, which has a great coffee set-up there (*The Deck on the Go*) with chalet-style shelters and heaters for the colder months. They are open every day except Monday and do a range of drinks and snacks.

After the marina you come to the blue Southbourne Sea Scouts building, where there is a small public car park by the path (PO10 8HS but it only takes around 6 cars). Take the path to the left, which leads to what looks like a private drive with ornate iron gates but is a public right-of-way. The drive curves to the left, and the path you want carries straight on along the gravel track, bringing you out to a field. Stick to the right-edge until you reach the road (Thorney Road), cross, then head across the field where you come out at the back of the black beach chalets on stilts. Follow the path to the right behind these chalets and you get back to the boat yard. Re-trace your initial steps back to the car park in Emsworth.

Benches: Some

Picnic Areas: None

Pubs: The Lord Raglan, The Coal Exchange

Public Toilets: West Beach

Cafes: Deck on the Go (x2)

Shops: in Emsworth

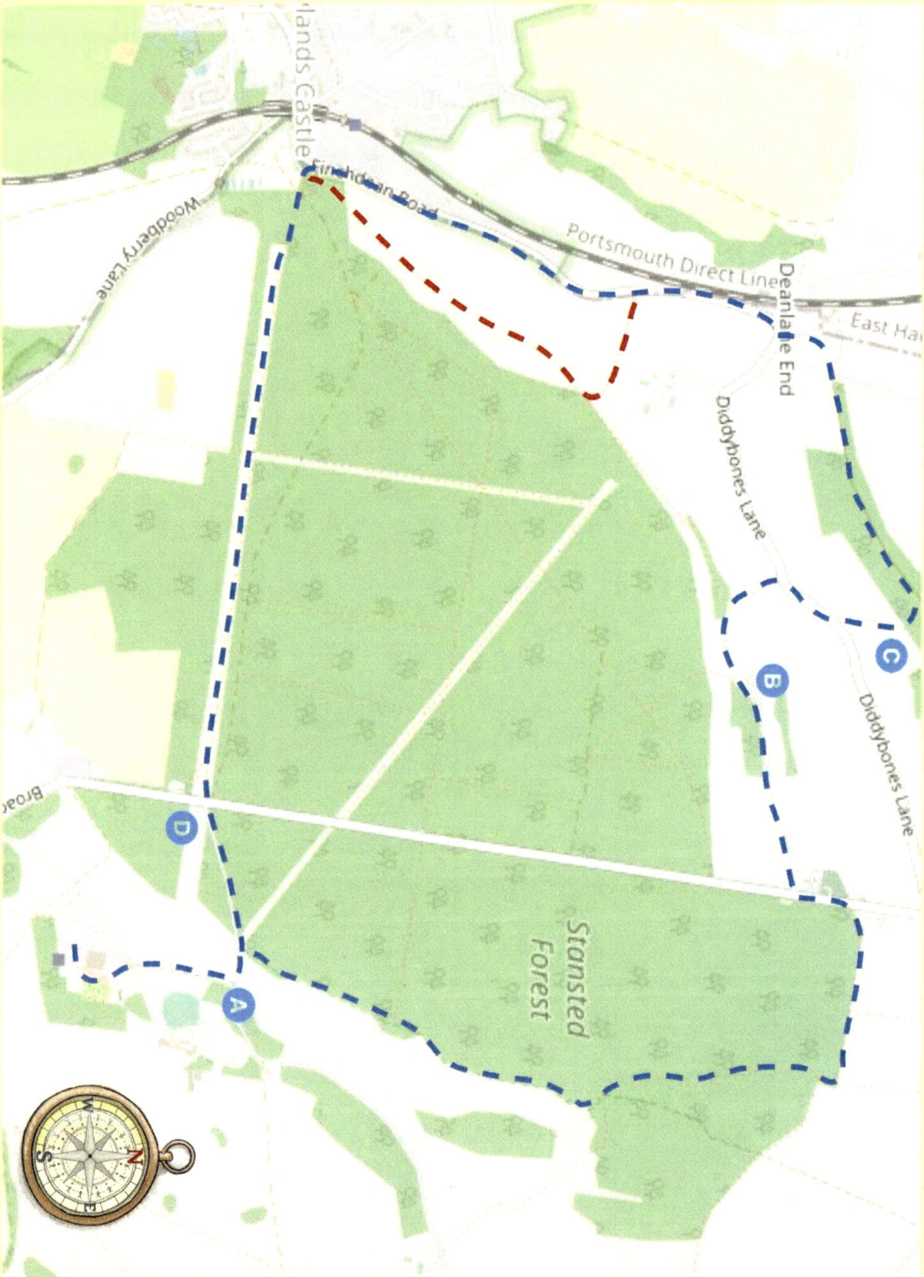

Finchdean Road
Portsmouth Direct Line
Deanlane End
Woodberry Lane
Diddybones Lane
Diddybones Lane
Stansted Forest
A
B
C
D
N
S
E
W

E4. Stansted Park

7 Miles   2.5 Hours   505 Ft Ascent

Pavement, Trail, and Road

Parking: Stansted Park, PO9 6DX (Free Parking open 8am to 5pm)

Bus: 27 From Emsworth to Rowlands Castle

Nearest Train Station: Rowlands Castle (.25 Miles from route, not Stansted House)

Starting from the Stansted House car park, head out of the car park using the exit road (bending to the left away from the garden centre) until you reach the road that leads to the house. Head that way, then just before the gate is a path leading off to the left, follow this until you reach the road, so the house is on your right, and you can look down *'The Avenue'* on the left.

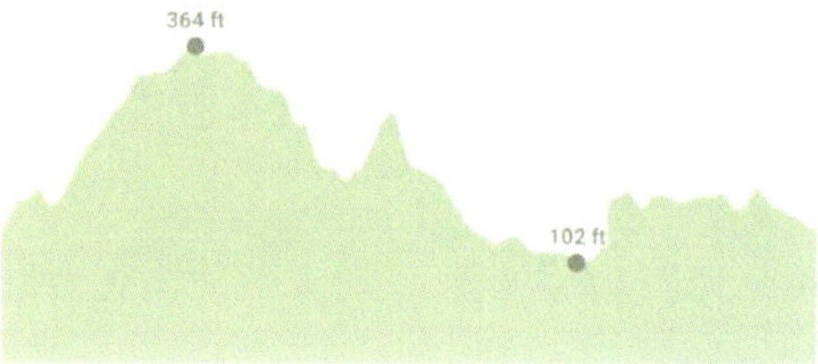

A At the road, turn left, and just after the speedbumps is a gate and track on your right at the edge of the woodland, signed as a public bridleway. This path takes you along the edge of the woodland, and in spring you have stunning displays of bluebells and foxgloves (*left*). You will go through a metal gate and at the edge of the field where the woods join is a clearing where paths intersect. Take the left fork, and the path that goes into the woods (signposted as a footpath rather than the bridleway).

In the woods, the path bears left and then right - there are signposts and markers, but they may be slightly obscured. Eventually you come to a path with a gate into a field ahead. Turn left here so you are passing the northern edge of the forest with fields on your right – as with all old forest paths there are lots of roots sticking out, so mind your footing! When you reach the road - Broad Walk - turn left, passing Christchurch Forestside (*below*).

The church is relatively new, constructed in 1852, and was built by the then owner of Stansted House Charles Dixon for his estate workers and the nearby village. The unusual design of the top window on the Eastern side is called a *'traceried mandorla'* and is designed to look like a leaf.

Just after the church is a gravel path on the right, signposted Warren Down Cottages. This will lead you past several paddocks (please don't feed the horses here) and continue along this until you get to a gate just before a cottage - the gate is usually open so you may find yourself walking down to the cottage before you realise it.

B Just in front of the gate is a path in the grass to the left, the signpost for which is hidden by the trees behind you. Take this path, which can be a bit overgrown, until you come out into a field. Keep straight across the field until you get to a gate, and you should see the path leading up the field ahead. NB – there is a path in the trees to the left here, but this gets very overgrown so I don't recommend it unless you have plenty of layers on.

Walk up the field until you reach Finchdean Road, where you have to walk on the road for a short stretch, so please take care. Just after the second property on the left you will see a signposted track between two of the houses leading to another field. Cross following the telegraph poles (watch out for cows and bulls in this field) to the gate. The track then takes you downhill until you reach a crossroads with a thatched cottage to one side (*left*).

C Take the left-hand trail, past another set off farm buildings, until you come out on

Finchdean Road, which is also part of the *Shipwrights Way*. Take the road to the right, but follow it as it curves left, following the line of the railway and signposted towards '*Rowlands Castle*'. The path winds and bends a bit but stay on it until you reach a hard-right bend. Opposite the bend, in the brick wall, you should see a gap with a footpath leading through it.

There are multiple paths that meet, but one is signposted the '*Monarch's Way*', and this is what you will follow back to Stansted House. It goes past a large tree in the centre of the path (*main picture*) until it brings you out on '*The Avenue*', which is a large open area lined with trees.

This was commissioned on January 29th, 1820, to mark the death of King George III, and when you reach Middle Lodge there is a commemorative plaque on the wall. The Avenue, from this point to the road, is just over a mile long, and to the house it is a mile-and-a-half. Head along the avenue until you reach Broad Walk (the church you passed is further back up this road), keeping to the left of the treeline, and when you cross take the service road to the right of the lodge.

D It is marked as private but for walkers it is still a publicly accessible path. This road takes you back to the speedbumps where you turned off, and on your right is the signposted path taking you back to the car park.

By the car park, you have a garden centre, a farm shop, and just inside is a café, with inside and outside seating that specialises in cream teas. The Bessborough Arboretum is of late Victorian origin, and includes Giant Redwoods, Paperbark Maple, Australian Shining Gum, and Foxglove Trees – the Stansted House website has a trail you can download and print off for the Arboretum. There is also a miniature railway and a circular maze here, but the opening times vary depending on the season.

There is a '*manor of Stansted*' recorded in 1327, but a hunting lodge is recorded here in 1177 when Henry II visited, and Richard I and King John hunted boar here. There have been several houses here, but the main block was destroyed by fire in 1900, though the stables survived. The main building was rebuilt in 1903, based on the footprint of the previous structure. In 1983, the 10th Earl of Bessborough set up the Stansted Park Foundation to run and maintain the estate as he had no male heirs (this was a few years ago, times have moved on!), and it is effectively a public concern.

You can visit the house if it is open (please check the website first), costing £10 for adults, and they run many events throughout the year both in the house and the grounds. In 2022, for example, they held a garden show, a nostalgia show, a summer jamboree, plays, and a prom.

Benches: Only by Stansted Tearooms

Picnic Areas: Only by Stansted Tearooms

Pubs: The Castle Inn, The Robin Hood (both in Rowlands Castle)

Public Toilets: Only by Stansted Tearooms

Cafes: Stansted Tearooms, The Bumblebee Cafe (Rowlands Castle)

Shops: Stansted Farm Shop

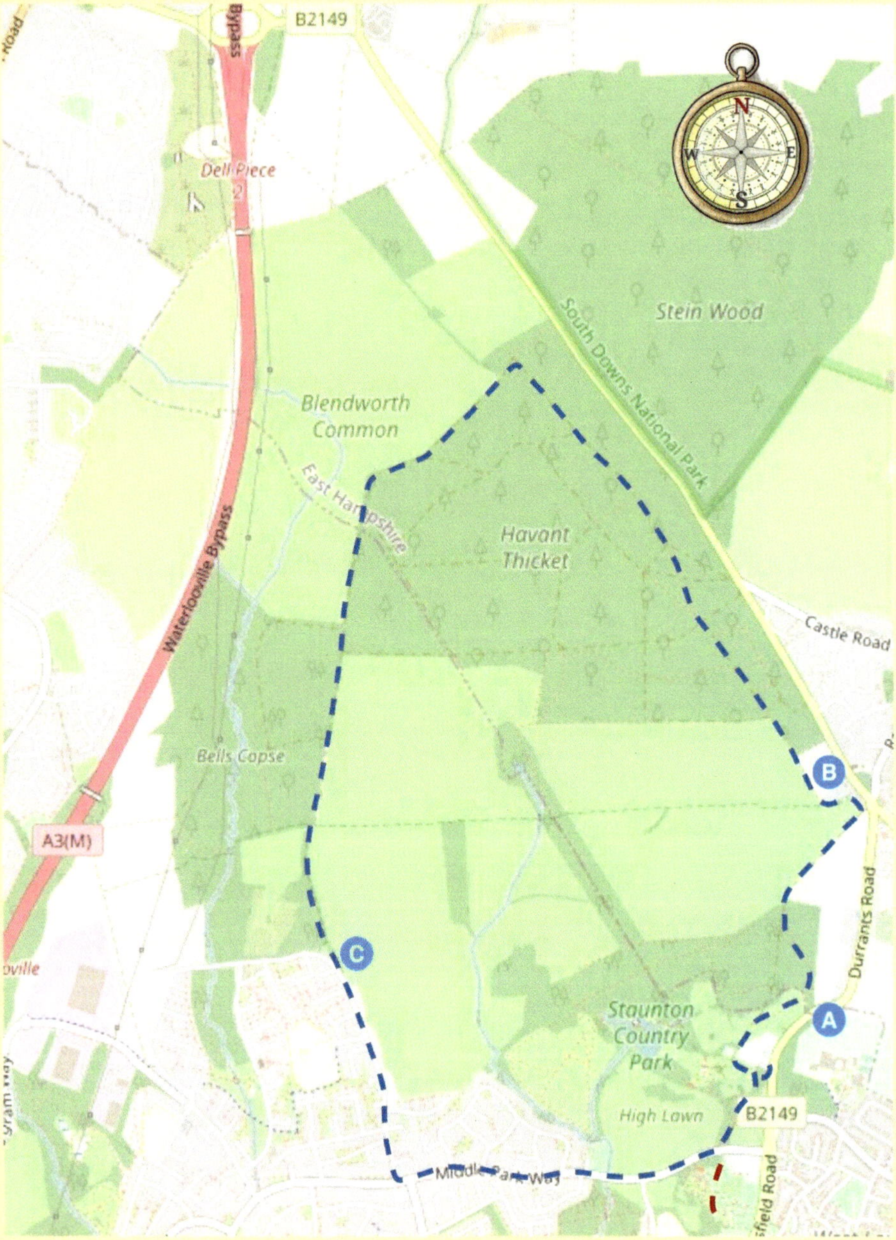

B2149
Dell Piece
Stein Wood
South Downs National Park
Blendworth Common
East Hampshire
Havant Thicket
Waterlooville Bypass
Castle Road
Bells Copse
B
A3(M)
Durrants Road
C
Staunton Country Park
A
High Lawn
B2149
Middle Park Way

E5. Staunton Country Park

5 Miles | 1 Hour 45 Mins | 270 Ft Ascent

All pavement

Parking: Staunton Country Park, PO9 5HD (£6 for 4 hours peak times, free if you visit Staunton Farm)

Bus: 20 or 21 to Staunton Park or Wakefords Way

Nearest Train Station: Havant (2 Miles)

Staunton Country Park covers the remains of an estate purchased in 1820 by the politician George Thomas Staunton (1781-1859). The City of Portsmouth bought the site in 1944, becoming a Country Park in 1987 (the main house was demolished in 1959). The site has been an area of contention recently as the heart of the park has been designated to become a new reservoir, flooding around 160 hectares to provide a new water source. Some steps have been taken to mitigate the environmental impact, but there will be a loss of grazing land and trees.

This walk takes you around the path that will mostly be the edge of the new reservoir, and one section takes you past houses, though if the new landscaping work has been completed there will be a path in place to avoid them. There are two car parks, one at the park and one at the farm, and if you visit the farm you can get a code for free parking which works at either site.

The park has several pre-marked walking paths, and this walk uses two of them to get a decent length, starting from the main car park. Head out of the car park by the parking pay meters and turn right joining the main path. A short distance ahead is a crossroads, with various trails indicated on it. For the first section we are going to take the light-blue trail, so head to your right, passing the play area. Along the path you will come to a gate on the right, marked by the blue arrow.

A This takes you into a field with '*The Beacon*' in it; a folly built in 1830 in the style of an ionic temple (*right*). Follow the path through the field in front of and to the left of the folly, to another gate. The path goes through the undergrowth and re-joins the main track you were just on.

Keep following the path until you reach a metal gate where you bear left, following the signs, without going through it. If you want refreshments, go through to the main road, where the Staunton Arms Harvester pub is. Follow the trail along straight until you reach a crossroads where you now take the purple trail going to the right (you can go through the woods ahead if you want to be a bit more adventurous, but the path is not always clear).

B When you get to the gate by the main road, take the purple path dipping down to the left of it and follow this trail for the next two miles as it loops around the top of the park and back down. Once you have looped round, the path comes to a fork with bridleway markings, the track you want curves to the left, where shortly afterwards you come to the edge of a housing estate.

C If the reservoir has been completed, the path will continue to your left, bringing you south of the lake until you reach the café. If the reservoir is still under construction, follow Swanmore Road round to the left as it heads down until you reach the T-junction with Middle Park Way. Turning left takes you back to the park, and half a mile ahead is the southern entrance of the park. Here you can turn left to go to the main café or take the path opposite to visit the farm and/or the farm shop. Tickets for the farm are £9.50 for adults and £7.50 for children, but there are combined tickets available. Food for the animals is £1 a tub and you can feed the goats (*above*), sheep, and llamas, as well as other animals there. There is also a maze, a herb garden, and a café inside.

Benches: Only in the southern area

Picnic Areas: BBQ and bench areas

Pubs: Staunton Arms

Public Toilets: By the cafe and farm

Cafes: Two

Shops: By the main café, farm shop by the farm

Gosport Area

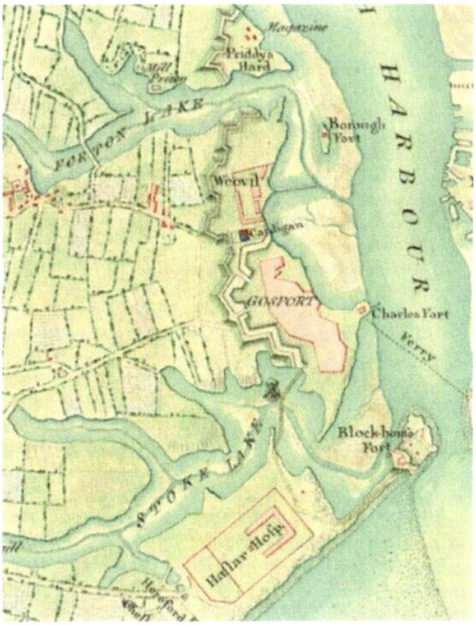

There are three theories as to the origin of the name *'Gosport'*, and locals will tell you which one they prefer, which tends to be the one of *'Gods Port'*, which is also the slogan on the town's emblem.

As the Royal Navy developed the landscape of Portsmouth, so too did they affect Gosport. The building of various forts to protect the harbour and the dockyards, such as Fort James and Fort Charles (c1678), was an early step. Large amounts of land were dedicated to the military subsequently - the Royal Haslar Hospital from the late 1740's, Priddy's Hard in the 1750's, and the Royal Clarence Yard victualling yard in the 1820's (which incorporated existing breweries, cooperages, and storehouses). All this required protection as well, resulting in the additions of bastions, barracks, and gun emplacements. As technological changes increased the range of artillery pieces, forts were built further and further away from the sites they were defending. This map on the right, from 1782, shows how much land was used by the MOD.

Though Gosport was influenced by the presence of the naval base in Portsmouth, it developed its own characteristics and personality. They had the new-fangled railway before Portsmouth, and Queen Victoria had her own station built at Clarence Yard to make it easier for her to get to the ships that would take her to Osborne House on the Isle of Wight. When she died, it was to Gosport her body was brought before being transferred to London. Part of the station building, at Victoria Quay, still exists but is not accessible to the public, though you can see it through the fence if you are nearby.

Burrow Island, in the harbour, has many tales attached to it, being the former location of Fort James. Many nowadays know it as *'Rat Island'*, from when it was used to bury deceased prisoners of war who had been kept on prison hulks in the harbour. The legend goes that when they ran out of space to bury the bodies they were just dumped onto the island, attracting large numbers of rats. There have been recent archaeological excavations on the site, with bones being recovered, but please note it is still MOD property and no public access is allowed.

During the English Civil War (1642-1646), when Royalist Portsmouth was holding out against the Parliamentarians, the Parliamentarians bombarded Portsmouth from the Gosport side.

Storing large amounts of gunpowder, and later cordite, always presents problems, and there have been several accidents affecting the area, such as in 1883 (*below*), and a large explosion in 1950. As recently as 2022, unexploded shells were found in Priddy's Hard which required the bomb squad to come in to defuse them.

A. Present Appearance of the Building.—B. Earth Mound Between the Manufactory and the Magazine.—C. The Shell Magazine.—D, Debris Thrown on to the Roof of the Magazine by the Force of the Explosion.

THE FATAL EXPLOSION AT A SHELL MANUFACTORY AT GOSPORT

In recent years, the MOD has been selling off land for redevelopment, with new housing at the Royal Clarence Yard, the Royal Haslar Hospital, and others. Some attempts have been made to keep a modicum of the character and history of these places, but if you get a chance to do any of the guided walks on the heritage weeks, I thoroughly recommend taking advantage of the knowledge of the guides who run them.

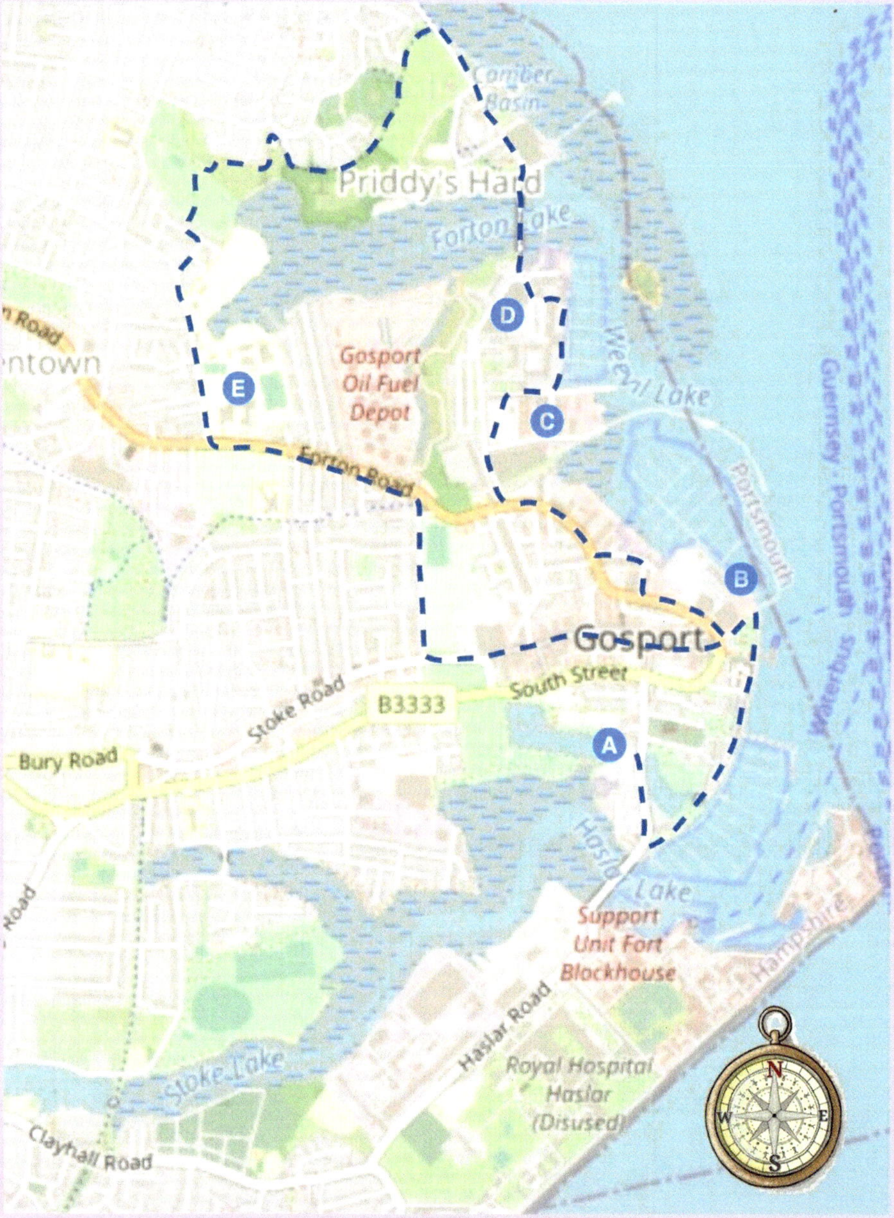
Camber Basin
Priddy's Hard
Forton Lake
D
E
Gosport Oil Fuel Depot
Weevil Lake
C
Forton Road
Portsmouth
B
Gosport
South Street
Stoke Road
B3333
Bury Road
A
Guernsey - Portsmouth
Waterbus
Haslar Lake
Support Unit Fort Blockhouse
Hampshire
Haslar Road
Royal Hospital Haslar (Disused)
Stoke Lake
Clayhall Road
N
W
E
S

G1. Supplying the Navy

5.25 Miles | 2 Hours 30 Mins | 16 Ft Ascent

Pavement and gravel tracks

Parking: Walpole Car Park, PO12 1NH (Pay, £1 per hour), Explosion! Museum, PO12 4LE (free, when open)

Bus: Any to Gosport bus station

Nearest Train Station: Portsmouth Harbour (take the Gosport ferry across)

Like Portsmouth (walk **P1**), Gosport has a '*Waterfront Trail*' of its own to follow, which this walk uses as a base. There is an annotated map of the full trail available from www.discovergosport.co.uk in their '*See & Do – Walks*' section.

A Starting from Walpole car park (so you are facing the bastion), turn right out of the entrance and walk along Haslar Road past Haslar Marina. Just before Haslar Bridge, there is a path on the left that takes you onto the trail. If you want to visit the National Museum of the Royal Navy's Submarine Museum (highly recommended), then carry on across the bridge and the entrance is on the left. When you have finished there, return to this point.

The path takes you to the harbour path, where there is the chain motif to follow (*main picture*). You get decent views across the harbour to Portsmouth, including Spice Island and Warrior 1860, as well as the new aircraft carriers if either of them are in port. On this side, you will pass the bus station on

B your left and the Gosport ferry on your right, then the Falkland memorial gardens.

The trail takes you to the main road, where you pass the Castle Tavern. Note the pub sign shows Portchester Castle, which is incorrect as it was named after Fort Charles, built here around 1678. Follow the trail past the chandlery and turn right down Harbour Road (the trail does disappear here for a bit, then re-appears at the end of Harbour Road). The trail leads to your left, taking you back to the main road, then along to Weevil Lane and the large white building that was formerly part of St. George Barracks. Note, Weevil Lane does not get its name from the insect; before the victualling yards there used to be a farm here owned by a man named '*Weovill*'.

Heading along Weevil Lane, you are now entering the area that was the heart of the victualling yards to supply the Royal Navy at its peak. Watch for an entry on your right to Cooperage Green, which has a large map of the buildings on the wall nearby. Though the trail continues ahead, we will go through the Green (which is now a car park) but look at the map on the wall to get an idea of the scale of the workings that used to be here.

C Go through the entry into Cooperage Green to the left of the map, then head diagonally across so the Pump House is on your left side (this Grade II listed building dates from 1778 and is now a café). Head between the buildings on the north side and you emerge onto Flagstaff Green, where the original Weevil House had stood since 1704. Between 1828 and 1832 these yards were all redeveloped and renamed the '*Royal Clarence Victualling Yard*' (after the Duke of Clarence). After the Second World War, the facilities here were gradually closed, with the Yard completely closed in 1991.

On your right, after the building with the cupola on the top, head to the bollards until you reach the marina. Walk along the promenade (*above*), and under the buildings until you get to the far end. These buildings were the granary and the bakery, and if you go into the restaurant on the left you can find the original brick ovens used for baking the bread for the ships of the Royal Navy. The building at the far end of the promenade, which is now a gym, was the storehouse with the slaughterhouse square alongside.

When you get to the gym building, turn left and head into North Meadow, another car park area between the buildings (you can park for free here, but there are only a few spaces and they go quickly.

D In the far corner are the studios for the marine artist Colin M Baxter (*left*). The studio is open Monday to Friday, and it is worth popping in both to see his work and to pick his brains. He has studied the area and its links to the Royal Navy and is happy to chat.

Now go out of the area to the north side - signposted *'Explosion!'* - and you cross the Forton Lake Millennium Bridge (I don't really need to say when this was built). Follow the road through the Explosion! Museum, which you can visit and has a café on the days it is open (check their website, but generally not Mondays or Tuesdays in winter months).

This area is known as Priddy's Hard and was originally constructed as a fortified position to help protect the harbour in 1750, but it became the main gunpowder store in the area in 1777 as the Square Tower in Old Portsmouth was too close to the civilian population. It ceased being used by the Navy in 1988 and the museum opened in 2001 – though there must be something about old gunpowder stores as, like the Square Tower, the site is a popular wedding venue.

Leaving the site through the north gate, stay by the coast for a few hundred feet and in the field on your left is a gravel path by a bin. Take this path, taking lefts at each junction until you get to Grove Road Recreation Ground. Here, take the left path so you come out at the housing estate. Turn left , take the first right, and you come out onto Mill Lane. Turn left and stay on this road, passing St. Vincent College, until you reach Forton Road (the A32).

E The college site was originally Forton Military Hospital in 1797, becoming an army barracks in 1808, and opening as a secondary school in 1975. It became a college in 1987, and if you are passing on the last Friday of the month and it is term-time there is a small museum inside you can visit to see the history of the site.

When you reach Forton Road, turn left, passing the college and the storage tanks of the Gosport Oil Fuel Depot (which supplies the MOD), then turn right down Spring Garden Lane. Keep an eye to the buildings on the right as you will pass the remains of the old train station (which has been converted into flats, *below and also Page 120*), which opened in 1841 but closed to passengers in 1953 and goods in 1969.

At the end of Spring Garden Lane, turn left (heading towards Morrisons), then walk through the paved main street for Gosport. On your left is the recently re-developed Gosport Museum. When you reach the Gosport Ferry again, turn right, and make your way back to the starting car park.

Benches: Only along the promenade

Picnic Areas: Grove Road Recreation Area

Pubs: Plenty

Public Toilets: By the cafe and the farm

Cafes: Plenty

Shops: Plenty

A
B
C
D
Gilkicker Point
River Alver
Bay House School Playing Field
Bay House School
Stanley Park
Privett
Alverstoke
Anglesey
Clayhall
Anglesey Road
Jellicoe Avenue
Bay Road
Gomer Lane
Broadsands Drive
St Helen's Road
Privett Road
Bury Road
Bury Hall Lane
Stokes Bay Road
Fort Road
Clayhall Road
Monckton Road
Haslar Road
Stoke Lake
Workhouse Lake
Gosport Park
Rectory Allotments
Clayhall Royal Naval Cemetery
Monckton Playing Fields
Institute of Naval Medicine
Fort Monckton (Military Training Establishment)
Gosport & Stokes Bay Golf Course
QinetiQ Haslar Marine Technology Park
Royal Hospital Haslar (Disused)
Support Unit Fort Blockhouse
Haslar Lake
Walpole Park
Newtown
South Street
Stoke Road
Portsmouth

G2. Following the Coast

6.75 Miles | 3 Hours | 16 Ft Ascent

Pavement, track, beach

Parking: Walpole Car Park, PO12 1NH (Pay, £1 per hour)

Bus: Any to Gosport bus station

Nearest Train Station: Portsmouth Harbour (take the Gosport ferry across)

Starting from the car park, go back to the main road then turn right onto Haslar Road. Cross the bridge - which gives you great views of HMS Alliance at the Submarine Museum (*main picture*) – and stay on this road.

As you walk past the old walls you get a feel for just how big the military sites in this area were at their peak. On your left you pass the entrance to Fort Blockhouse, which has protected this side of the entrance to Portsmouth Harbour since 1431, though it has undergone many changes over the years (*right, viewed from the harbour*). It was extensively rebuilt under Charles II and became the Fort Blockhouse Submarine Mining Establishment in 1877. The large white tower you can see in the background of the main picture was the Submarine Escape Training Tank, which opened in 1954 and was used to train submariners in how to escape their vessels. It closed in 2020, with the training being re-located to Faslane, Scotland.

A Behind the wall on the left lies the site of the Royal Hospital Haslar which, when it opened in 1753, was the largest brick building in Europe. Being built on the peninsula, patients could be kept inside, both to prevent disease spreading to the general populace and to keep pressed men from escaping. It was heavily used during the Napoleonic and World Wars - especially D-Day with the country's first blood bank being established here. It closed fully in 2009.

Behind the walls on the right was the Gunboat Yard from 1856 to 1906. It also took on a role as part of *HMS Hornet* (coastal forces), and then part of the Admiralty Small Craft Experimental Works. Also on this site, in 1886, the world's first water-tank for testing ship designs was constructed.

When you get to the end of Haslar Road, turn left onto Clayhall Road and then left again onto Dolphin Way (marked '*England Coast Path*'), which opens out onto great views of Portsmouth Harbour. Turn right, heading to Fort Monckton, where you have to take the path right, through the car park, then join Fort Road (there is no public path through the golf course that is now here).

B Stay on Fort Road until you reach the gate for Fort Gilkicker (*left*) which was completed in 1871 to provide extra coastal defence, but was recently sold and is likely to be developed into (expensive) flats. At the fort, take the path to the right and stay with the coast all the way until you reach Battery Number 2 and the Diving Museum (*right*).

There are two cafes on this section: Pebbles, which has a café (9-5 in summer) and a bar area (12-3 and 5.30-9 in summer), and the Bayside Cabin Café (8-6). You also pass a splash park for the kids, and near the end on the right is a decent sized green for picnics (no tables there though) and games such as frisbee. There are also public toilets by the Diving Museum.

C The Diving Museum is a little gem, and well worth a visit, though it only opens at weekends and bank holidays (11-4) between April and October. It is worth visiting, and you may be surprised at the equipment that was used to explore the depths of the sea.

Follow the road as it curves past the Diving Museum to the right, then head left at the roundabout. A short way along, cross the river Alver (*left*), an take the trail alongside it. Head up here to Privett Road (which is the bottom end of walk **G4**, the Alver Valley) and turn right.

Stay on Privett Road past the two roundabouts (passing the Cocked Hat pub on your left, which is a decent place for refreshments) and it turns into Bury Road. You pass the Gosport War Memorial Hospital on the left, the foundation stone for which was laid in 1921 by Field Marshall Earl Haig and opened in 1923.

Carry on along Bury Road, ignoring side roads, until it bends to the right as Foster Road (ahead of you should be a sign saying, '*Welcome to Stoke Road Shopping Area*'. Take the road right, turn left onto South Street at the end, then take the second-right, Prince Alfred Street, which takes you down to Workhouse Lake.

D Workhouse Lake (originally known as Alver Creek) is named for the large workhouse that used to be present by the bridge on the opposite side (*below, where the new builds are*). It was operational from 1801 until just after World War II. You get a good amount of birdlife in the two areas you pass now, including cormorants (*right*) and grebes.

Follow this road past the lake, between the houses all the way to the gas tanks at the end, where you turn left at the new build houses (so the large blue gas tank is on your left). This leads you out to Gosport Park, where there is a play area and a café. To get back to the starting car park, just follow the shoreline.

Benches: Only along the coast path

Picnic Areas: Walpole Park, Stokes Bay

Pubs: Plenty

Public Toilets: By No 2 Battery

Cafes: Pebbles and Bayside Cabin (Stokes Bay)

Shops: Some near the end

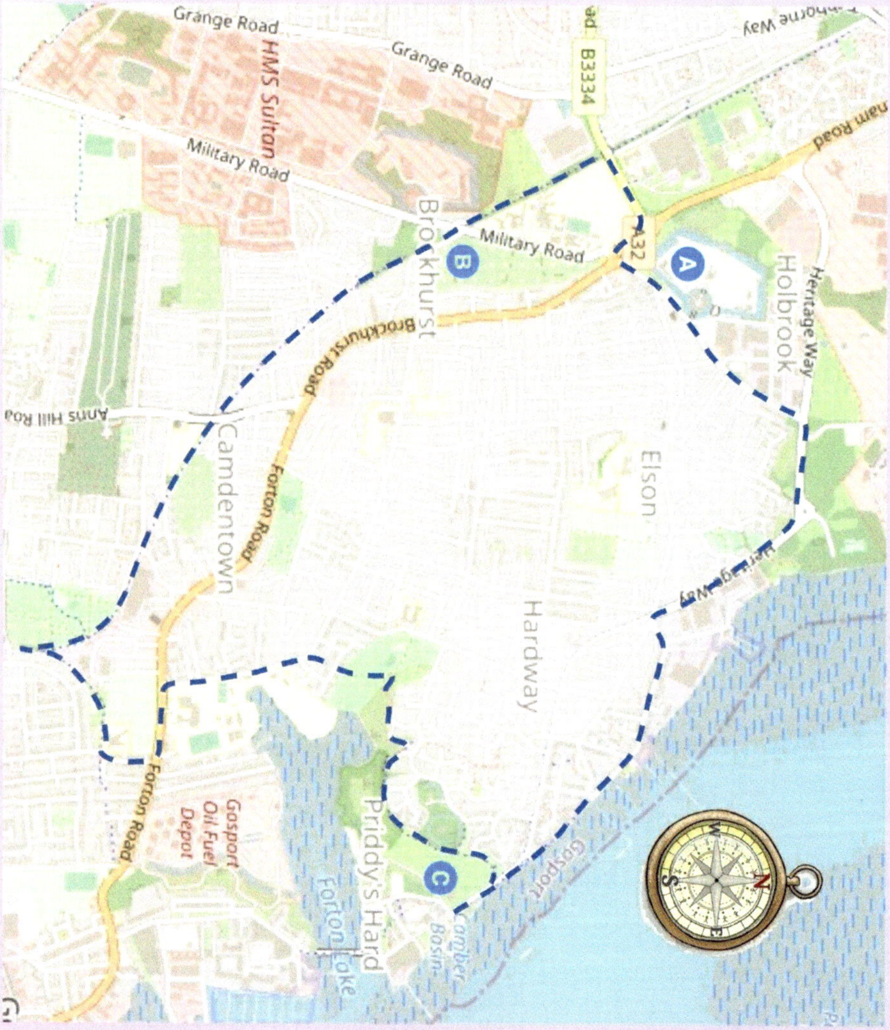
Grange Road
Grange Road
HMS Sultan
Military Road
Military Road
B3334
A32
Brockhurst
Brockhurst Road
Holbrook
Heritage Way
Anns Hill Road
Camdentown
Forton Road
Elson
Heritage Way
Hardway
Forton Road
Gosport Oil Fuel Depot
Priddy's Hard
Forton Lake
Camber Basin
Gosport
A
B
C
N
S
W
E

G3. Forts and Trains

5.25 Miles | 2 Hours | 25 Ft Ascent

All pavement

Parking: Explosion! Museum (Free), PO12 4LE

Bus: Fort Brockhurst (E1)

Nearest Train Station: Portsmouth Harbour (1.5 miles + ferry)

A relatively short stroll, this one takes in part of the England Coast Path, and then uses the walking/cycling route of the railway that used to be in Gosport. It is flat all the way and is suitable for wheelchairs.

Starting at the Explosion! Museum, where there is a café if you want to refresh yourself at the end, head north (away from Gosport) out of the complex and along Heritage Way (*right*). Pass the Jolly Roger Pub, and you reach the Hardway Memorial, which was built to commemorate the loading of troops for D-Day from this spot. Go onto Priory Road and past the Old House at Home until you reach the large junction. Go right, up Heritage Way, and stay on this, keeping left at the next roundabout, until you get to Gunners Way - this takes you down past Fort Brockhurst (*main picture*).

A Fort Brockhurst, built between 1858 and 1862, was one of the five Gosport ones built to protect Portsmouth Dockyard if England was invaded further along the coast. Like the other Palmerston Follies, by the time they were completed they were pretty much pointless as artillery ranges had greatly increased, meaning shells could be lobbed over the top of them to reach the navy's infrastructure. It was used as a training base, being decommissioned in 1957, and is now maintained by English Heritage and opens occasionally to the public – you may want to call English Heritage to ask when it is open next on 0370 333 1181 when planning this walk.

Walk past the Fort to the next junction and cross the main road to the right of the bus stop. On the other side, head right for a few yards then left along Rowner Road (the B3334). There is a gentle climb as the road goes over Henry Cort Way, which is the path you want, so take the stairs (or ramp) down to it on the right. Go under the bridge (*above*) and follow it back towards Gosport.

The last passenger train to travel this route was on June 6th, 1953, and it was re-purposed in places as a bus route, with this section for walkers and cyclists opening in 2012. Henry Cort (1740-1800, *right*), who the route is named after, originally worked in London as a Royal Navy Pay Agent (one who collects officer's pay and pensions on behalf of his clients). The uncle of his second wife inherited an ironmongery concern in Gosport which Cort took over the running of. Cort spent time - and Royal Navy money - improving the refining of the cast iron produced for the likes of chains and anchors used by the Navy. Unfortunately for him, the Navy seized his property when he could not pay them their money back.

B When you reach the road junction, cross, and go down Station Road, and re-join the cycle route a little ahead on the left. Note the building on your right as you pass - it is the old station house, and you can still see the platforms in their garden.

Cross Lees Lane, with the path continuing along the side of Carlyle Road. You then pass a skate park on your right, then a wall made of shipping containers on your left. After the containers the path splits, take the one to your left that curves round to a park (Kings Road Play Area) and then Newtown C of E Primary School. Directly after the school, head left up Albert Street. This takes you to Forton Road (the A32) where you turn left past St Vincent College. This section is also covered in walk **G1**, see Page 105 for some detail on the college.

After the college go right along Mill Lane until you reach the two stone-clad houses at a junction. Go right along St Vincent Road, left at the end, and you will see the entrance to Grove Road Recreation Ground. At the path junction in the park, take the right fork back to Explosion! where you started.

C The ramparts outside of the Explosion! Museum (*above*) occasionally open to the public, especially with the assistance of the Portsmouth & Gosport History Group Volunteers. They run a week every August where they hold open days, talks, and more across the area, bringing the local history to life (www.portsmouthgosporthistory.com).

When you get back to the museum car park, there is a café at the back of it, giving you great views of the harbour and the ships that are in (*above*) – you can use the café without having a museum ticket and there are toilets there.

If you look out into the harbour, you can see a platform with two lowered crane arms – unless they are loading a ship in which case the cranes will be raised. It is here that Royal Navy ships have their live ordnance loaded, rather than doing it too close to the ammunition stores at Bedenham (further north from your current position) or in the dockyard. Live ammunition is shipped to this platform, then the warships come alongside to load (or unload if returning from duty).

You may also see some older warships at anchor to the left of the bay, anything here is waiting to be disposed of, whether for scrap or sold on to another nation.

Benches: Only along the coast path

Picnic Areas: Grove Road Recreation Area

Pubs: The Jolly Roger, The Old House at Home

Public Toilets: None

Cafes: Explosion!

Shops: None

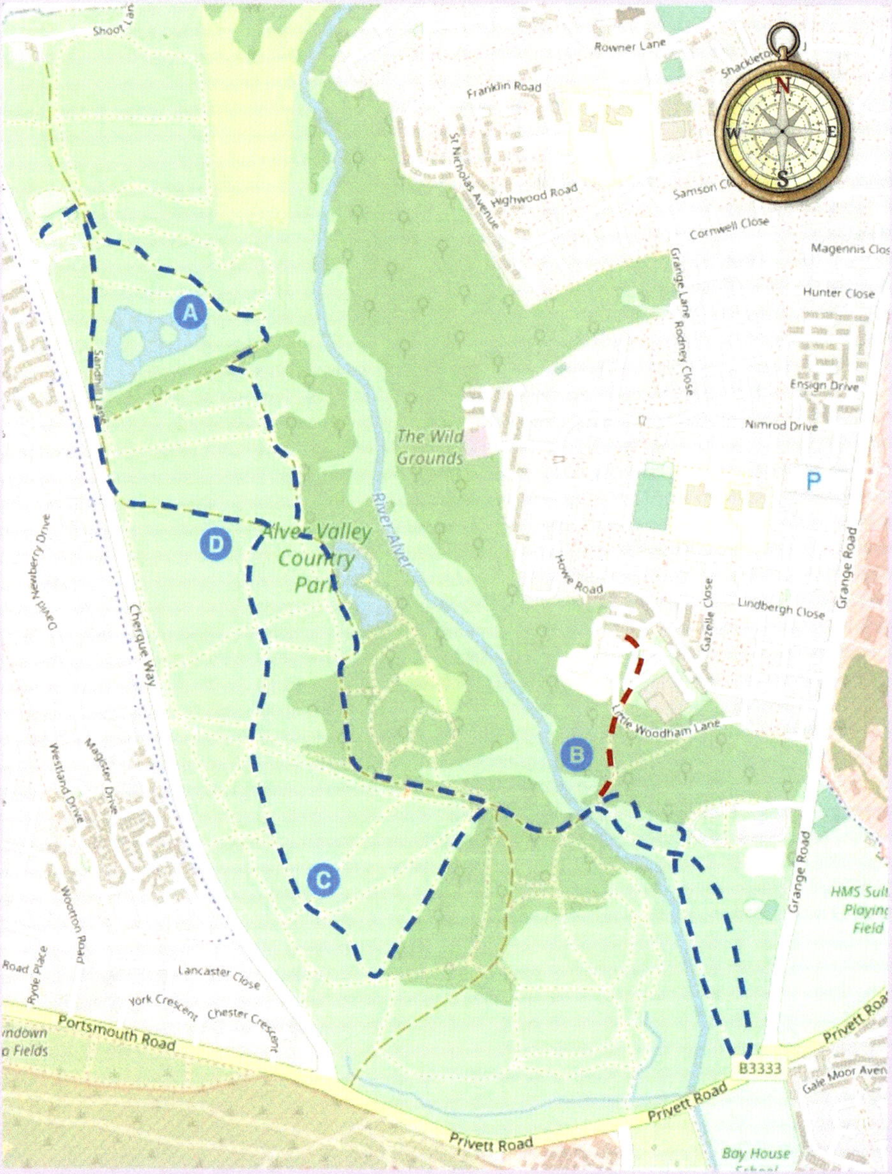

Shoot Lane
Rowner Lane
Franklin Road
St Nicholas Avenue
Highwood Road
Cornwell Close
Hunter Close
Grange Lane
Rodney Close
Ensign Drive
Nimrod Drive
N
E
S
W
A
B
C
D
P
The Wild Grounds
Alver Valley Country Park
River Alver
Sandhill Lane
Cherque Way
David Newberry Drive
Howe Road
Gazelle Close
Lindbergh Close
Grange Road
Little Woodham Lane
Westland Drive
Magister Drive
Wootton Road
Ryde Place
Lancaster Close
York Crescent
Chester Crescent
Portsmouth Road
Privett Road
B3333
Bay House

G4. Alver Valley Country Park

3.75 Miles | 1 Hour 30 Mins | 20 Ft Ascent

Gravel, Tarmac, and Grass

Parking: Alver Valley (Pay, £1 per hour), PO13 8BH, Alver Valley East (Pay, £1 per hour), PO13 8AS

Bus: North-East, Lee-on-the-Solent Community Centre, X5, West, Grange Road, 9, 9A

Nearest Train Station: Fareham (4 Miles)

Alver Valley Country Park is an oft missed haven, having fields, trees, lakes, and a stream, as well as old fortifications tucked away for you to find. There is a large play area and a skate park for the kids, and though it is right alongside the centre of Gosport you feel isolated from the hustle and bustle. There are great views of the Solent and the Isle of Wight from a couple of the viewpoints, and many trails criss-cross the park for you to explore at your own leisure. In one corner of the park there is Little Woodham (PO13 8NZ), the Seventeenth Century Village Experience, which brings to life the year 1642 (used as a filming location for *Doctor Who* and several historical documentaries).

This walk goes past both car parks, though I usually start at Alver Valley West (rather than Alver Valley East) as it tends to be quieter. You will go through the park in a clockwise direction, sticking to the main trails, so you can familiarise yourself with the area before getting adventurous and discovering the other trails.

Take the trail out of the car park (by the information board) and after a few feet it joins the main track (Sandhill Lane), take a left, then one hundred feet later take the gravel track on the right. This bends round (so you are going back on yourself) and follow it until you reach Noah Lake (*right*).

A There is a viewing spot here if you want to go down and feed the ducks and swans (remembering to feed them grain, peas, oats, or corn, not bread).

Continuing along the path past the lake, you enter some trees, then cross a marshy area using zig-zag wooden boards (*left*). The path curves up to the right, where there is a junction with a large wooden post in the centre of the fork. Take the left fork until you reach a T-junction with the main access road. Bear left onto this road, passing fields and then through more trees. You pass several tracks leading off into the woods – these do all join up but for this walk stay on the main path.

B The path curves to the left and goes to Apple Dumpling Bridge (*below*), and there is an information board explaining the possible origins of the name. Cross the bridge and head up the narrow tarmac track directly ahead (ignoring the road to the right) - you are now climbing up the remains of a small motte and bailey castle. It was probably a 12th Century construction, but there has been little or no documented excavation work done on it.

A short way up the path it splits into three. Take the right turning into the woods and follow until you reach the red brick structure, which is a Type 26 pillbox built to protect the military airfield that used to be to the north-east of here. Go round the pillbox and follow the path as it drops back down to the right to a marshy area, then carry along to the main road. Just before the car park (Alver Valley East) with the metal barrier, take the gravel path off the road to the right. When you reach the T-junction of two paths, head left along the river Alver, following it almost all the way to Privett Road at the southern end. Slightly before you

reach the road, there is a grass track curving back on you to your left, which takes you back to the East car park. Keep to the right path when it splits, which takes you past the picnic tables and another play area. I've included this section along the river as there is the opportunity to see kingfishers and other birds amongst the reeds and trees (*right, a European Green woodpecker, below, common red soldier beetles on cow parsley*).

When you reach the car park, take the main track back over Apple Dumpling Bridge (ahead to the left) until you come out of the trees to where a series of trails meet (there is also a bench and a bin here). Take the gravel path on the left after the bench and then the left fork in the grass. Follow this until you reach a stile on the left with the '*MOD Training Area*' warning sign. On your right there is path leading up the hill, which takes you to a stone bench at the top.

C This is a great viewing spot, you can see Portsdown Hill, the Spinnaker Tower, and across the Solent to the Isle of Wight. If you are lucky you may see some of the vintage aircraft, such as a Spitfire or Harvard flying out of Solent Airport - the aircraft used in Christopher Nolan's *Dunkirk* film were based at the airport in 2017 and were regularly seen flying over the area. The airport was initially part of the Royal Naval Air Service and used for training pilots for seaplanes in 1917, though it then became an RAF base for a while. In 1939, the airport became HQ for the RAF Coastal Area, becoming HMS Daedalus in 1939 as the Fleet Air Arm came under Admiralty control. It is now a commercial airport for small aircraft, though the Coastguard still operate from there as well.

D Continue along the path as it dips down, then up another small bank, keeping straight until you reach a bench. Ahead, the path then takes you back to the main access road, keep to the right when it forks, and turn left onto the access road where it curves back to the car park where you started. It is worth taking this road rather than the trails as there is a hide along the way where you can view Noah Lake.

The café in the West car park opens every day between 8 a.m. and 6 p.m., though you may find these hours are reduced during the winter months. There are toilets at the back of the café and a large play area here with a giant slide (*main picture*) and zip wires.

Little Woodham (*next page*), at the edge of the park, is a 17th Century Living Village and there are signs for it in the park. It only opens two weekends a month, so please check their website first, and costs £5 for adults and £4 for children.

Benches: Around the park

Picnic Areas: Take a blanket

Pubs: The Wyvern, The Cocked Hat, both 10 minutes walk from the park

Public Toilets: At the main car park (not East car park)

Cafes: West car park (not East car park)

Shops: None

Little Woodham (PO13 8NZ), the 17th Century village run by the Gosport Living History Society, on the edge of Alver Valley Country Park.

www.littlewoodham.org.uk

Right, Master Christopher in the Grey Goose Weavers.

West of Portsea Island

There are several areas to the west of Portsmouth that are great for walking, giving you the options of coast, river, or downs. Gosport to Warsash for the coast, the River Meon and the Titchfield Canal for your waterside walks, and the Meon Valley Trail leading onto the South Downs Way is a great place to begin your explorations.

The Titchfield Canal was built in the 17th Century to irrigate the water meadows from the river Meon, and as well as the water meadows and the nature reserve, there are the remains of Titchfield Abbey to visit. The abbey is free, with the remains a mix of the original 13th Century monastery and later 16th Century buildings.

The Meon Valley Trail (*above, in early Spring*) is based on the railway line that ran between Fareham and Alton and was used to transport produce. The total length of the available trail is 11 miles (one-way), running from Wickham to West Meon. There are car parks at each end (PO17 5HY for Wickham and GU32 1HS for the West Meon end), but these can get busy at weekends.

The track itself is in good condition, though can get a little muddy in winter, and is used by walkers, joggers, cyclists, and horse-riders. It was a double-track railway so is wide enough to be able to keep your distance from people, and benches are positioned every couple of miles, as well as plenty of old tree stumps and logs to use as seats if you need to take a breather.

Most of the trail is within the boundaries of the South Downs National Park and there is a plethora of fauna and flora you can spot: deer, red kites and buzzards, kingfishers, rabbits, foxes, fungi (*above*), and more. There are a few information boards along the trail, and it has a multitude of paths leading off it if you want to explore the area some more (Ordnance Survey Explorer Map 119 covers these offshoots).

Wickham, at the base of the Meon Valley Trail, is built around the old fording point of the Roman Road that ran from Chichester to Winchester, and in 1334 was worth more to the crown in taxes than Fareham.

It had good-sized tanning and brewing industries based there in the 18th and 19th centuries, aided by the ready supply of fresh water. Chesapeake Mill was built in 1820, and is constructed out of the timbers of an American ship, the *USS Chesapeake*, captured by the Royal Navy in the War of 1812. The mill is now an antiques store with a small café. Another naval link is to that of *HMS Prince*, whose captain at the Battle of Trafalgar in 1805, Sir Richard Grindall, is buried in the churchyard of St. Nicholas (*right*).

Gosport Railway Terminus, circa 1844

Titchfield Abbey circa 1784

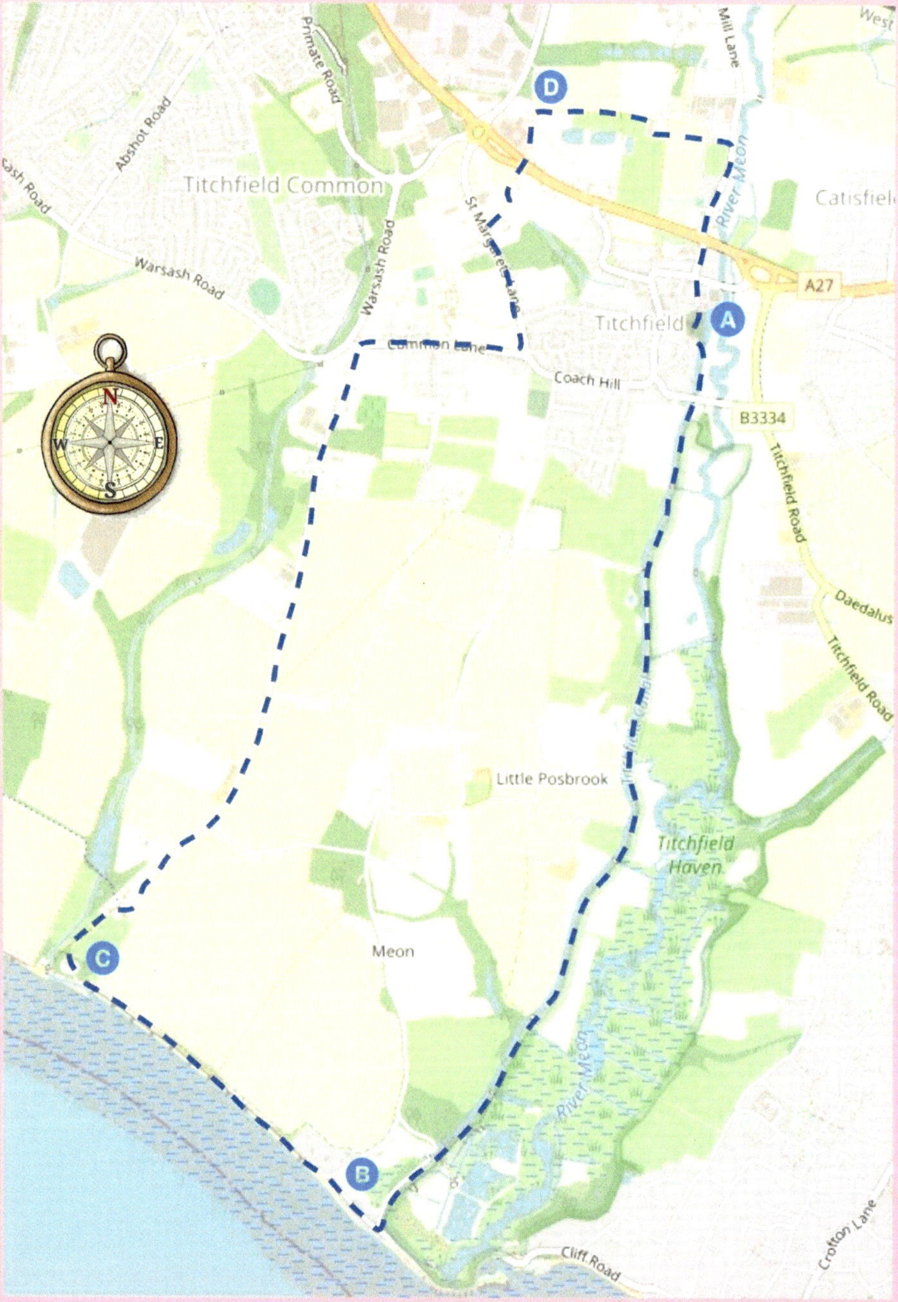

Primate Road
Mill Lane
West
Absshot Road
D
Titchfield Common
River Meon
Catisfield
St Margaret's Lane
Warsash Road
Warsash Road
A27
A
Titchfield
Common Lane
Coach Hill
B3334
Titchfield Road
Daedalus
Titchfield Road
Little Posbrook
Titchfield Haven
C
Meon
River Meon
B
Cliff Road
Crofton Lane
N
E
S
W

W1. Titchfield Canal and Abbey

7.5 Miles | 2.5 Hours | 142 Ft Ascent

Pavement, trail, one section of Road

Parking: Titchfield Recreation Ground Car Park (free), PO15 5RD,
Meon Shore Car Park (free), PO14 4HN
Bus: Mill Lane/Primary School, 604 from Fareham, 609 from Paulsgrove
Nearest Train Station: Fareham (2 Miles)

This walk takes you down Titchfield Canal to Titchfield Haven Beach, then back up passing through farmland. The end of the route brings you to Titchfield Abbey, where there are a couple of decent pubs for refreshments or a meal. It is important to note that in wet weather and Winter, this can get quite muddy and flooded, so you may want to save it for drier days.

From the Recreation Ground car park, turn right and head to the main road, crossing it and heading down Mill Street on the other side. At the end of Mill Street, turn left onto East Street, then a right down Church Path. This takes you into the grounds of St Peters Church (*above*), which still has Saxon stonework visible inside, especially over the chancel arch. It was extended in 1180 and in the 13th Century, with the wealth and status of the area boosted by Titchfield Abbey. Though the church was restored in 1866, inside are plenty of older traces, including the somewhat excessive *Southampton Monument*, dating from 1594 and created by the Flemish sculptor Gerard Johnson.

A As you walk through the graveyard, there is a path with a low wall in front of it, take a left, crossing the bridge, then follow the path to the right alongside the remains of the Titchfield Canal all the way down to the beach. It is not a 'canal' in the way you would associate with barges and narrowboats but was used to feed water meadows using a series of sluices. There are still areas of contention on the usage of this watercourse, but the evidence points to an agricultural rather than transport origin. Most of the fields you pass on the left are protected breeding areas for birds, so if you have a dog with you then please ensure they don't cross into these areas (*above*).

B At the far end of the canal (about 2 miles along), is a gate where there is a road ahead and a path that drops down to the left. Take the path, following it round the edge of Titchfield Haven Nature Reserve until you see the toilet block by the beach on your right. We will come off the path here, but if you want to explore the nature reserve, or use the café there, carry on to the entrance. When you are ready, come back to this point. The wildlife in this area is fantastic, including buzzards, deer, and banded damselflies (*below*).

Cross the road, then turn to your right where there is a gate and path heading between the beach chalets – you need to walk along the road for about 30 feet to get there. The public footpath leads between the chalets, so follow it through until you do a dogleg left then right, which heads up a small climb between the gorse bushes. This track you are following is part of the '*Solent Way*', a 60-mile path leading from Milford on Sea to Emsworth Harbour.

Stay on this trail until you reach a junction, where you head left and keep on, ignoring turn offs into the fields away from the coast. If the weather is fine there are great views from here of Norris Castle on the Isle of Wight, and Fawley Refinery at Southampton.

C Continue along the path until it opens out and you come to signposts. Take the right-hand path, marked as a *Permissive Bridleway*, taking you behind the farm. When you reach the main track, Brownwich Lane, turn right and you will now follow this track up to Common Lane (about a mile-and-a-half). Part-way along, this track turns into a concrete path and curves to the left past the farm buildings, then it carries on north. There is a path in the trees to the right that follows alongside this track if you want to avoid traffic (though it is not a busy section), but make sure you do not take any of the side-branches; you want to keep heading straight north.

When you reach Common Lane, turn right, going past the school until you reach the junction with St Margaret's Lane, where you turn left. There is a short section ahead with no path, then you come to a white building on your right (*Tinkerbell's Creations*). There are signs for the footpath immediately after the building to the right. Follow this path as it goes through the trees, curving to the left at the fence. It brings you out into a field, where you keep to the right-hand edge to Southampton Road (the A27). Ahead of you on the other side is a public footpath, so cross and take this new track. It takes you past a new retirement estate (with the hotel on your left), until you reach the access road for the estate.

D To your right should be a security barrier, and ahead a grass track (with the estate on your right). Take the track and follow it until you reach Titchfield Great Barn (*above*).

The barn dates to around 1408-1411 and was used by the monks of Titchfield Abbey to store their tithe collections, though it has links to Henry V and there is speculation it was used (or planned to be used) as a storage point for supplies heading to France for what would become known as the '*Hundred Years War*'. It now hosts regular theatre events and weddings.

At the barn, the path jinks to your left, then right. Follow it past the garden centre until you reach Mill Lane again (just up from where you started). Turn left and enter Titchfield Abbey, then when you have explored, head back down Mill Lane to the car park.

Titchfield Abbey (open from 10-4 in winter and 10-5 in summer, free entry) was founded in 1222 for Premonstratensian canons. When Henry VIII had his spat with Rome (and needed funds for his wars), the abbey was closed and converted into an estate, known as Place House. In 1781, the then owners the Delme family decided to create a 'romantic ruin' and pulled down much of the later house. This exposed more of the older structures, and you can still see sections of medieval floor tiles.

Benches: Scarce

Picnic Areas: The Beach

Pubs: Titchfield Mill, Fisherman's Rest, The Wheatsheaf

Public Toilets: At the beach

Cafes: By Titchfield Haven Nature Reserve

Shops: None

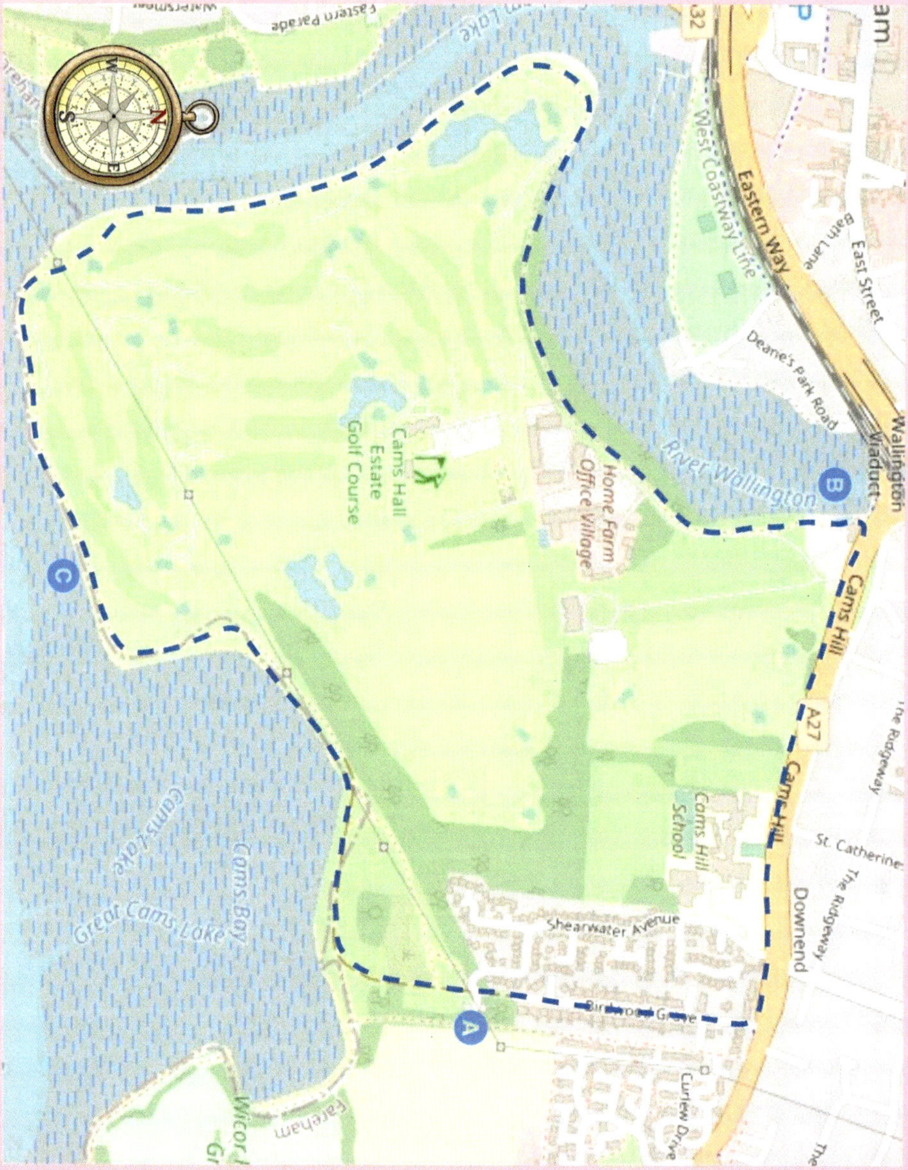

Cams Hall Estate Golf Course
Home Farm Office Village
River Wallington
Wallington Viaduct
Cams Hill
A27
Cams Hill School
Shearwater Avenue
Birdwood Grove
Curlew Drive
Downend
The Ridgeway
Deane's Park Road
Eastern Way
West Coastway Line
Bath Lane
East Street
Eastern Parade
Great Cams Lake
Cams Lake
Cams Bay
Fareham
A
B
C

W2. Cams Hall Walk #1

3.15 Miles | **1 Hour** | **95 Ft Ascent**

Mainly gravel and dirt paths (boots recommended in winter), one stretch of pavement.

Parking: Cams Water Car Park (free), PO16 8YQ

Bus: Delme Arms, 3, F3, X4

Nearest Train Station: Fareham (1.25 Miles)

This is a nice, flat walk, with great views from Fareham Creek towards Portsmouth (*right*). It can get a little muddy in winter, but in summer and early autumn it should be fine for pushchairs and wheelchairs.

I tend to walk this loop anti-clockwise, as it is nicer to get the stretch of road and houses out of the way first, so the rest is purely Fareham Creek.

A Head north out of the car park and up Birdwood Grove until it reaches Portchester Road (the A27). Turn left and carry-on past Cams Hill School and the golf course. When you reach the Cams Mill pub (the Delme Arms is on the opposite side of the road), turn left after the pub so you get a good view of the railway viaduct, which was constructed in 1848 (*main picture*). Coming out from under the road bridge is the river Wallington, and this is where it meets Fareham Creek and feeds out into the Solent. This area is tidal, so you get different birdlife depending on the tides (check *KHM Portsmouth* website for tide times). There are always plenty of swans here if you have some grain to feed them (*remember, white bread is not recommended for feeding ducks and swans*).

B Follow the path past the pub towards the Cams Mill Business Estate, with the shoreline on your right. You will see a right fork that takes you into the trees, with the main estate on your left. This path now takes you back to the starting car park, with the golf course on your left and the creek on your right. The land here was registered to Earl Godwin in the Domesday Book (1086), with the current house (Cams Hall) built in the 1770's. The estate fell out of use over time and in 1950 a large explosion on the Bedenham ammunition piers (which you can see clearly on the longer **W3** Cams Hall walk) caused considerable damage to the area. In 1996, the estate buildings were rebuilt and extended, creating the business complex you see now.

C Keep following the path as it winds its way around Fareham Creek. On the opposite bank on your right, you should see a clear grassy area with a large orange windsock. This is part of Fleetlands, where they repair military helicopters and, if you are lucky, you may see a Chinook or a Merlin on a test flight.

Stay on the path until you come to the open area with benches, then there is a path on your left that leads back to the car park where you started.

Benches: A few, mainly near the car parks

Picnic Areas: 1, south of the main car park

Pubs: Cams Mill, Delme Arms

Public Toilets: None

Cafes: The Dovecote Eatery

Shops: None

Cams Hall, c1830

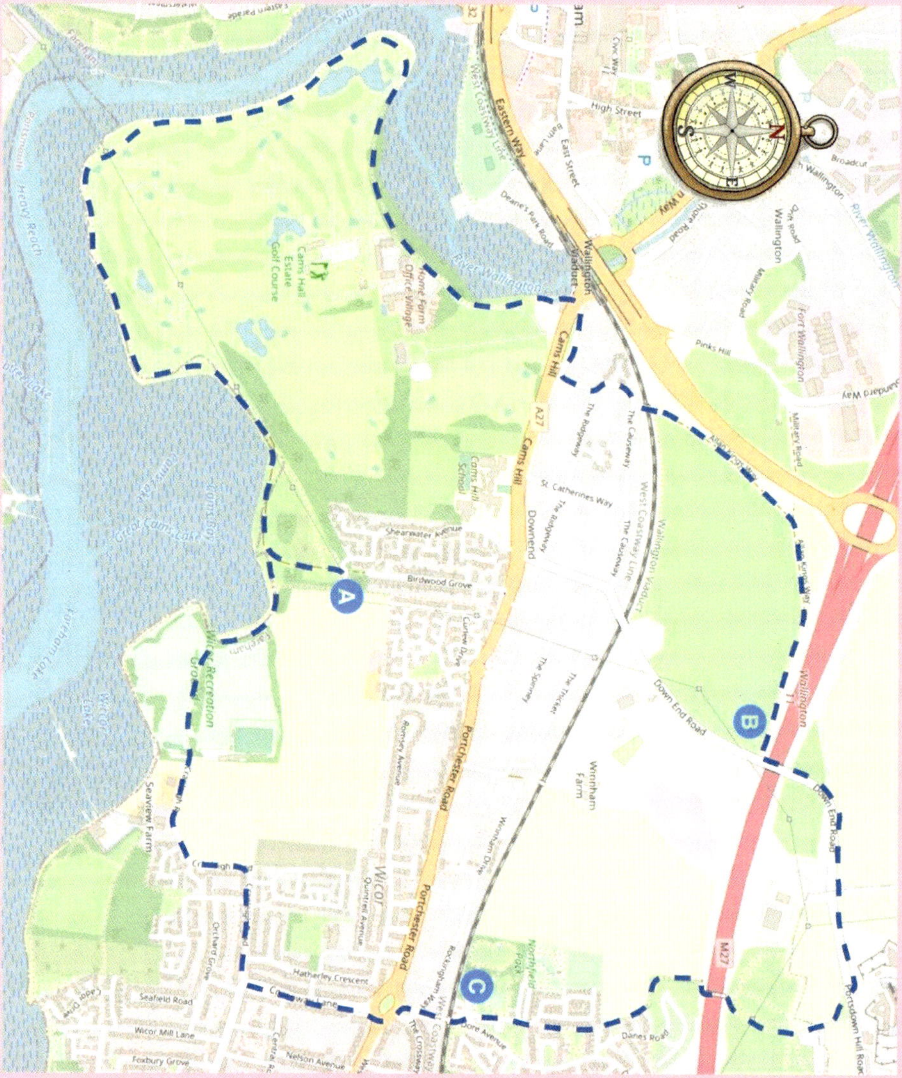
Cams Hall Estate Golf Course
Home Farm Office Village
River Wallington
Wallington Viaduct
Eastern Way
West Coastway Line
High Street
East Street
Deane's Park Road
Shore Road
Broadcut
Wallington
Military Road
Fort Wallington
Pinks Hill
Standard Way
Cams Hill
A27
Cams Hill School
The Ridgeway
The Causeway
St. Catherines Way
Downend
Wallington Viaduct
Shearwater Avenue
Birdwood Grove
Curlew Drive
Great Cams Lake
Cams Bay
Portsmouth Heavy Reach
Fareham Lake
Wicor Lake
Wicor Recreation Ground
Down End Road
The Spinney
The Thicket
Winham Farm
Romsey Avenue
Portchester Road
Winham Drive
Wicor
Quintrell Avenue
Seaview Farm
Orchard Grove
Hatherley Crescent
Seafield Road
Wicor Mill Lane
Foxbury Grove
Nelson Avenue
Rockingham Way
Northfield Park
Dore Avenue
Danes Road
Portsdown Hill Road
M27
A
B
C
N
S
E
W

6.15 Miles 2 Hours 305 Ft Ascent

Mainly gravel and dirt paths (boots recommended in winter), pavement, and one stretch of road.

Parking: Cams Water Car Park (free), PO16 8YQ, Wicor Recreation Ground (free), PO16 9BY

Bus: Delme Arms, 3, F3, X4

Nearest Train Station: Fareham (1.25 Miles)

This is an extension of the previous walk, but with Portsdown Hill and the café at Fort Nelson added for some great views, though we go clockwise this time rather than anti-clockwise.

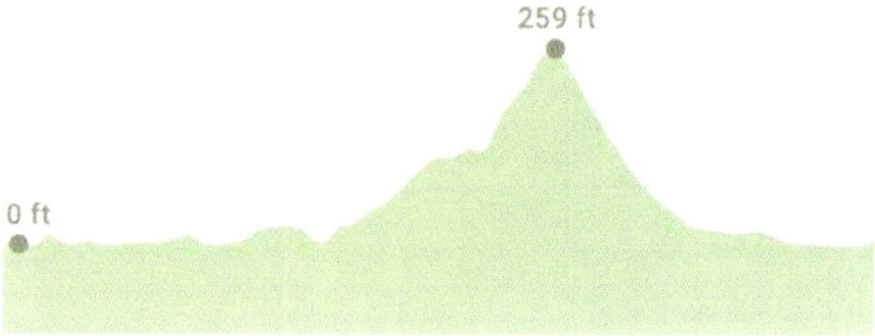

A From the carpark, walk south towards the shoreline, turn right and follow the path all the way to the Cams Mill pub. The shoreline will be on your left and the golf-course and estate on your right for this section of the walk.

When you reach the main road (the A27), cross-over and head right, up Cams Hill. The third turning on your left is a gravel track, Paradise Lane. Take this track, follow it to the end, and then go straight when you reach the next housing area. Paradise Lane continues in a straight line after the houses, then over the railway bridge, and along the fields until you reach a service road. Turn right at the track and stay with the hedge-line until you reach Downend Road and the bridge over the motorway.

B Turn left, crossing the bridge, and take the road to Fort Nelson car park (opposite the big guns). There is a short section here where the path is very narrow and it is easier to walk on the busy road, so please take care. At this point, you can visit Fort Nelson, which is free, and there is a café with some outdoor tables if the weather is nice.

Just before the car park, take the trail to your right leading downhill, and follow it past the car park. Stay on this track (don't take the right fork, though it looks tempting), which curves to the right and joins the footbridge over the motorway. Cross here, stop to admire the view (*above*) then at the end of the bridge take a dogleg to the right then left to take you down the track.

This track brings you out at Upper Cornaway Lane, where a path to the left crosses the field. At the end of the field, turn right again and continue heading downhill.

C When you reach the roundabout by the BP garage, use the underpass to cross and head down Cornaway Lane so the Seagull Pub is on your left. Follow this road until you reach a T-junction, where you turn right onto Cranleigh Road.

Cranleigh Road has a dogleg in it then you pass the small marine repair facilities. - there is the Salt Café down that lane if you want refreshments and great views. Continuing ahead, you come to Wicor Recreation Ground - there is a skate park here if you happened to have brought your boards with you!

Take the track across the fields (either side of the hedge-line) until you reach Fareham Creek. Turn to the right, then follow this track until you see the path to the starting car park off to your right.

Benches: Along the southern and west shore of the creek

Picnic Areas: 1, south of the car park

Pubs (3): Cams Mill, The Delme Arms, The Seagull

Public Toilets: None

Cafes: 2, Fort Nelson, Salt Cafe

Shops: 1, M&S at the BP garage

The Forts at Spithead, London Illustrated News, 1888

Part of Palmerston's Follies

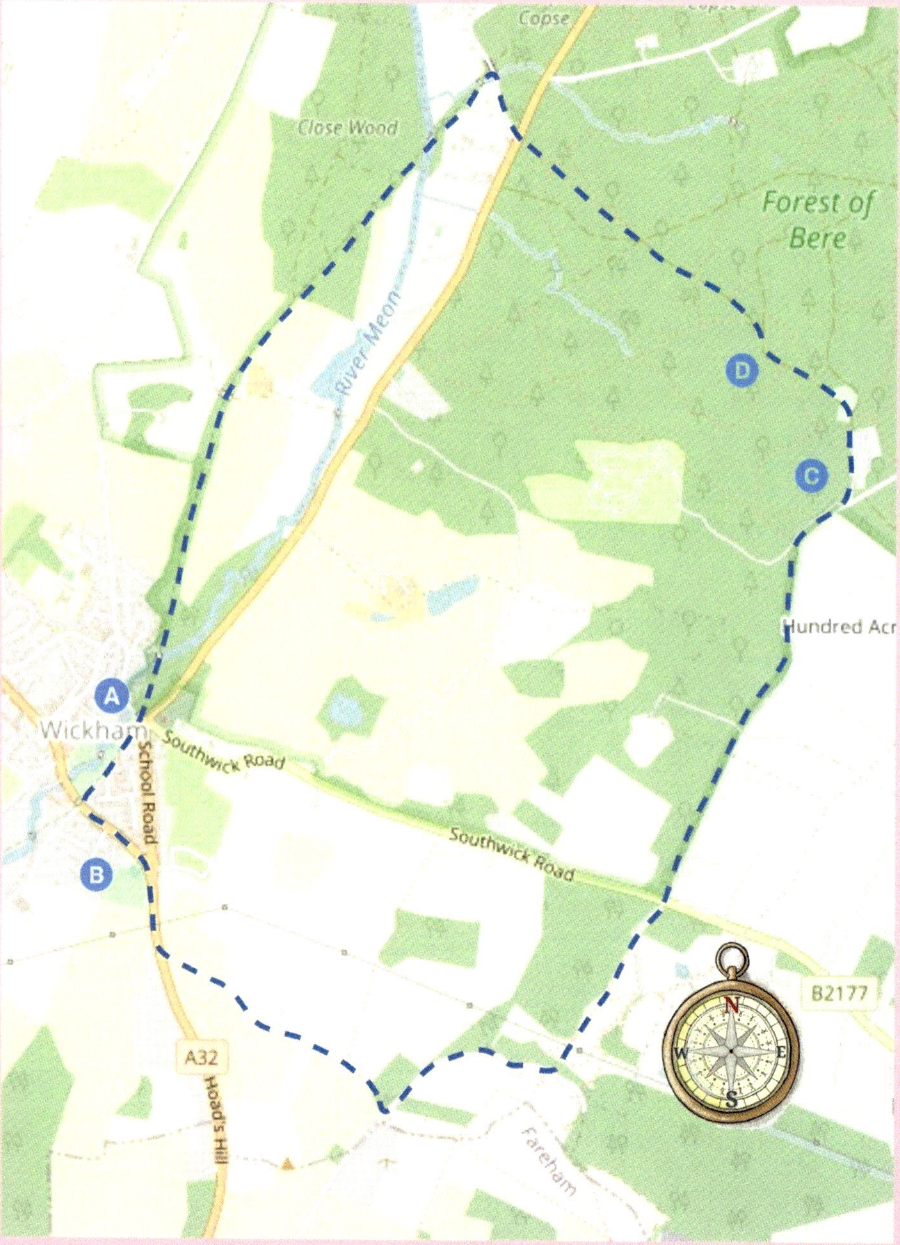
Copse
Close Wood
Forest of Bere
River Meon
D
C
Hundred Acr
A
Wickham
B
School Road
Southwick Road
Southwick Road
B2177
A32
Hoad's Hill
Fareham
N
W
E
S

W4. Meon Valley Walk #1

5.5 Miles | **1 Hour 45** | **320 Ft Ascent**

Mainly gravel and dirt paths (boots recommended in winter), one stretch of road.

Parking: Wickham Car Park, PO17 5HY (free), West Walk Car Park, PO17 6JD (Pay)

Bus: Wickham Square, 38, 69, 96, 691

Nearest Train Station: N/A

This walk is a good introduction to the Meon Valley Trail and West Walk, which is part of the Forest of Bere. It has a couple of picnic spots but please be aware there is a section where you must choose between a road with no footpaths or a bridleway that gets very muddy in wet weather, so it is not ideal if you have young children or dogs with you.

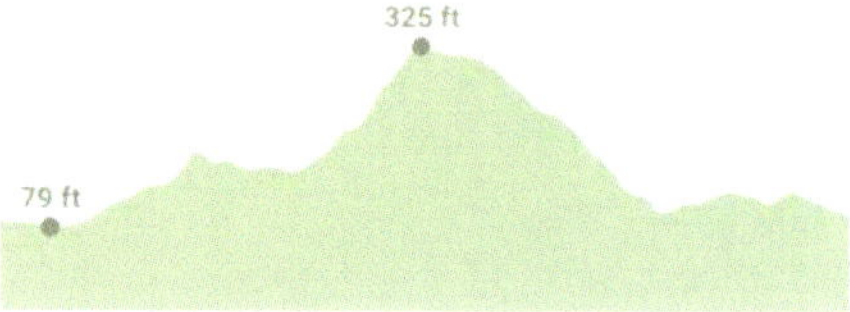

A Starting from the free car park in Wickham, go onto the Meon Valley Trail and head south, as if you are going into Wickham. Just down the trail, the trees on your left clear to give you a good view of St. Nicholas Church (*right*). It is believed there has been a church on this spot since before 670 A.D., and there are surviving Norman traces in the current building.

Carry on along the trail, and on the right is a path down to the Wickham Water Meadows, which are fed by the Meon River. This walk carries on straight ahead, but if you head down to the weir there are benches and a picnic area. Though the walkable area there is small, it is a very charming and peaceful place to visit and is a nice area to sit with a sandwich and listen to the water running through the weir.

B When you get to the bridge crossing the main road, head down off the trail to the left, and continue along the road towards the Shell garage. At the garage, cross to your right and head up the hill (towards Fareham). A few hundred yards up the road on your left is Castle Farm Lane. Cross the road and follow the lane until you reach a T-Junction with a modern cottage ahead (*left*). Head down the road to the left (Forest Lane), passing Meadow Farm, several other houses and a row of cottages. Just after a house on its own, Porch House, is a large silver gate on your left. Go through this, through the trees and out onto Wickham Common, keeping to the left side of the field.

At the far end of the field, you will come out onto a small road, turn left and follow this to the crossroads where the B2177 meets Hundred Acres Road. Now you must choose between the bridleway (potentially muddy) or the road. If you choose the road, please take reasonable precautions (with children, dogs, or headphones).

For the road option, follow it past the old brick enclosure wall on your left, and keep going until you reach the Forestry Commission car park.

If you take the bridleway, which runs parallel to the road on the left side just behind the trees, stay on it until you reach a service track (marked no public entry on the left). The path continues ahead to your left just before the gate, then continue until you reach a small road. Turn right onto road and follow it to the main road, where ahead on the left is the entry to the Forestry Commission car park (which is Pay & Display).

C Walk through the car park, passing the gate and another picnic area, until you reach a fork with a stand of trees between the two paths. Take the gravel path to the left and follow it until you reach another junction.

D Take the left fork (still a gravel path, *right*) and follow until you reach a junction where five paths meet. Take the narrower path immediately in front of you, and a short way along it on your left is a sign for the *Pilgrim's Trail*. Take this route and follow the trail signs until you reach the A32, with the Roebuck Inn in front of you. The Roebuck accepts walkers and dogs and is a good place for refreshments.

When you are ready to continue, head down the Kingsmead track to the right side of the pub. Follow it until you reach the bridge, where on the right you will see a path heading down to the track, going under the bridge. Take the track down, turning to your left so you pass under the bridge and are heading south. Stay on this track all the way back to the car park.

The forest you are walking through is a great place for spotting mushrooms, bluebells, and foxgloves, amongst others, and when it is quiet you should hear, and maybe see, woodpeckers in spring. The open areas of Wickham Common are ideal for spotting buzzards and red kites on warm days.

Also, don't forget to keep an eye out for pinecones, for as we all know they make great weather predictors (closed when damp, open when dry) for the kids to experiment with.

Benches: Wickham Recreation Ground, West Walk

Picnic Areas: 2

Pubs: The Roebuck Inn

Public Toilets: None

Cafes: None

Shops: BP Garage

Also in the area:

Chesapeake Mill, built from the timbers of a Georgian-era US warship, with café, PO17 5JH

Wickham Square, pubs, shops, PO17 5JT

Westlands Farm Shop, SO32 2JW

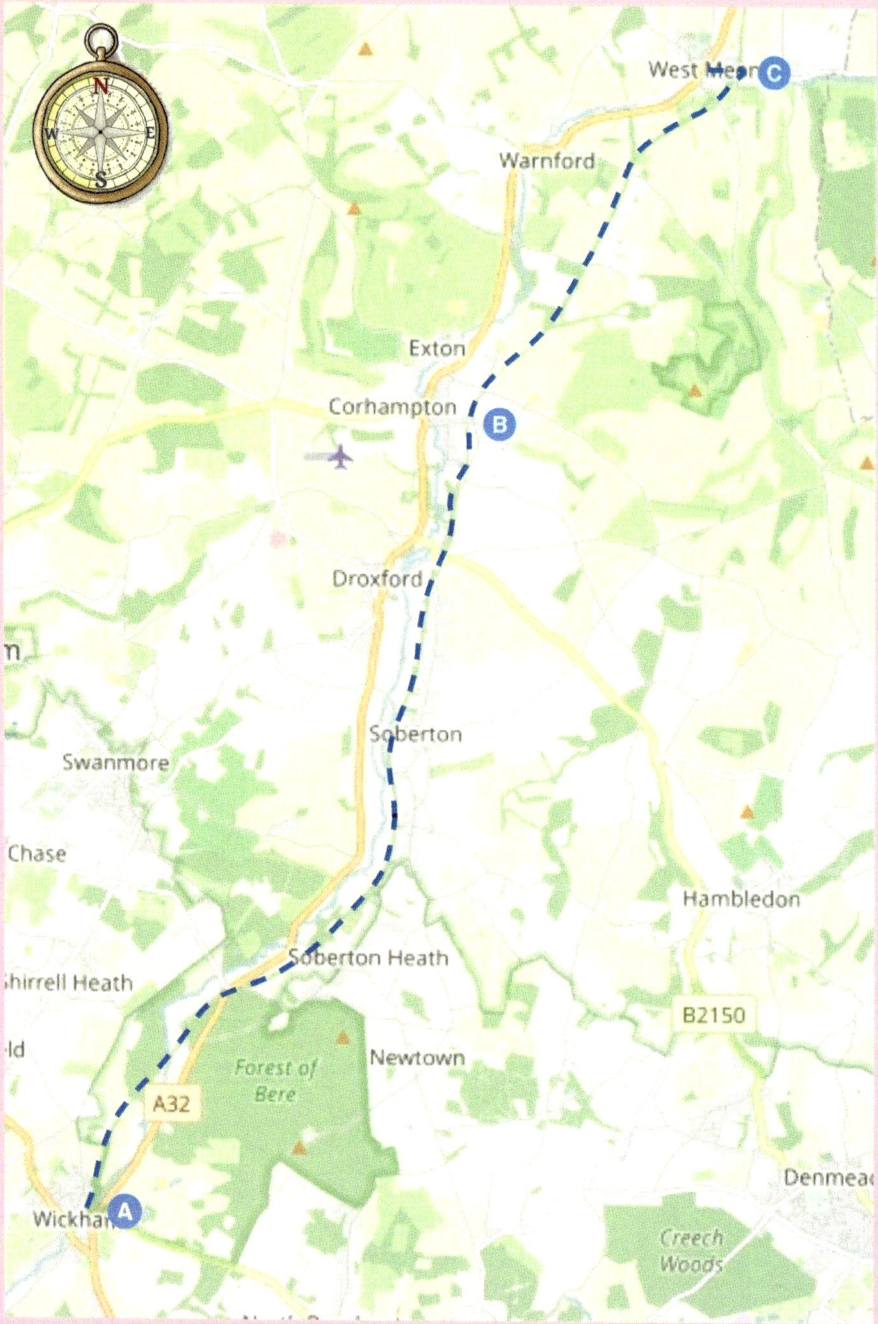
N
S
W
E
West Meon
C
Warnford
Exton
Corhampton
B
Droxford
Soberton
Swanmore
Chase
Hambledon
Soberton Heath
hirrell Heath
B2150
Newtown
Forest of Bere
A32
Denmead
A
Wickham
Creech Woods

W5. Meon Valley Walk #2 – There and Back Again...

19 Miles **7 Hours** **820 Ft Ascent**

Mainly gravel and dirt paths (boots recommended in winter), one stretch of pavement (the trail is suitable for bikes).

Parking: Wickham Car Park, PO17 5HY (free), Meon Valley Trail North Car Park, GU31 1HS (free)

Bus: Wickham Square, 38, 69, 96, 691

Nearest Train Station: N/A

This walk is not a loop, instead going from the car park in Wickham to the end of the Meon Valley Trail, where you can stop at the café or the pub for a drink and some food, and then back down the trail to where you started.

It is pretty much flat all the way, 820 feet of ascent over 19 miles is negligible, and most of the path is well protected by trees so it works well in the rain or on hotter days. I use it to see how my fitness levels are doing - if I can do the walk in under 6 hours in spring, then I am on track for longer walks in the summer.

A From the car park in Wickham, turn left (north) up the trail and follow it. 5 miles up the track you get to the turning for Droxford where, in 1944, Winston Churchill had an armoured car stationed in the sidings here whilst the preparations were underway for D-Day. Pass the old railway station, which is now a private residence, and the edge of the old platform to the north of the station makes a good place to sit and take a drink.

B *About 7 miles in, the track crosses the South Downs Way. If you want to get some hill walking in you could turn right and follow the trail up to the top of Old Winchester Hill, which has the remains of an iron age fort.*

Today though, keep going along the Meon Valley Trail and after a few more miles you reach the car park at the far end of the trail (GU32 1HS). There is a picnic area here should you want to rest, but it is not far to the pub and café. Continue on to the service road to the left as it heads downhill, following it until it meets Station Road, the main road.

On the opposite side of the road, a few yards to your left, is a small track. Head down it and follow it across the river Meon and up to the next road, the High Street.

C Turn left here, until you reach the pub and the café. Once you have refreshed yourself, turn round and head all the way back.

If you set off early in the morning, and the weather is good, you will likely see deer, rabbits, hares, buzzards and red kites on this walk. In spring, there are carpets of wild garlic and bluebells (*above*).

Benches: Roughly every 2 Miles

Picnic Areas: Near the top end of the trail

Pubs: The Thomas Lord

Public Toilets: None

Cafe/Shop: West Meon Village Shop

South of Portsea Island

Okay, so technically it is the Solent directly south of Portsea Island, but you have to cross the Solent at least once in your life, so what better way than to take the hovercraft across, walk around Ryde, and finish with a fish-and-chip supper?

During the Battle of the Solent, on the 18th and 19th of July 1545, Henry VIII watched his flagship, the *Mary Rose*, sink in the Solent. What is rarely reported is that on the 21st of July (probably) the French invaded the Isle of Wight. Their thinking was that if they could get a foothold on the island, their fleet would be in a much stronger position. The French landed troops in a couple of different places, including Bonchurch in the south-east corner. Reports of the battle vary, and there is no reliable primary source as to the outcome, but the local militia and the women put up a fierce fight, helping to resist the invaders. It is likely that a larger battle at Bembridge a few days later ultimately drove the French back to their ships.

If you do get a chance to visit the island, then make sure to visit the dinosaur museum in Sandown, and then go fossil hunting in the cliffs just south of the town (taking the utmost care around the cliffs). You can also take a guided fossil hunt with the experts from the museum.

When you get the ferry or hovercraft over, make sure to pick up one of the guides to the island, as you will be surprised at how much it has to offer. Despite how small the island looks from Portsmouth; it actually covers 148 square miles.

The Hovercraft coming into Portsmouth, with one of the car-ferries behind it and Clarence Pier on the right.

It's always great to see the hovercraft come in, and this is the only commercial hovercraft service running in the world. Sir Christopher Cockerell perfected the hovercraft, with the first of his designs being the SR.N1 (Saunders-Roe Nautical 1) which made its maiden '*flight*' in 1959. There is a hovercraft museum in Lee-on-the-Solent, by Gosport (www.hovercraft-museum.org, PO13 9NS) which is worth a visit if you have an interest in these wonderful machines.

A
B
C
D
Ryde
Esplanade
George Street
Union Street
Lind Street
West Street
High Street
B3330
A3054
Binstead Road
Binstead Hill
Quarr Hill
Pelhamfield
Ryde School with Upper Chine
Pellhurst Road
Mayfield Road
Greenmount Primary School
Ryde Academy
Ryde Golf Course
Binstead
Hamilton Road
Binstead Lodge Road
Newnham Road
Quarr Wood
Isle of Wight AONB
Fishbourne Copse
Binstead Airfield
Swanmore
Weeks
Ashey Road
Upton Road

S1. Ryde

6-7 Miles | 3 Hours | 535 Ft Ascent

Pavement, gravel and dirt paths, several stretches of quiet roads with no pavement, two fields

Parking: Fastcat, Gunwharf Quays PO1 3EF, Hovercraft the Esplanade Car Park PO5 3AD

Bus: The Hard (multiple options)

Nearest Train Station: Portsmouth Harbour

The length of this walk depends on the method of transport you take to get to the Isle of Wight. If you take the hovercraft, it is a little over 6 miles, if you take the passenger ferry and walk Ryde pier (main picture), it is a little over 7 miles. There are some sections at the start of this walk where there are no pavements, but they are quiet so it should not be a problem.

If you take the Fastcat from Portsmouth Harbour station, walk down to the end of the pier. If you take the hovercraft, turn right from the terminal so you are in front of the entrance to the pier. The pier is the world's oldest pleasure pier and is actually comprised of three piers. The main pier you can walk/drive down is the primary structure, opening in 1814. The middle, dilapidated pier (main picture) was the tramway which opened in 1864, and the third pier, which is now used for trains, opened in 1880. The railway on the Isle of Wight is peculiar in that it runs refurbished London Underground trains on its line.

A Standing with your back to the pier and looking at the shops and cafes, turn to your right and walk along St. Thomas Street, passing toilets and the beach on your right. After the car park on your right is Buckingham Road, turn right down here (signposted '*Coastal Path*') and follow it as it curves uphill to the left. When you reach the T-junction, turn right onto Spencer Road. Follow this for half-a-mile until you get to the junction with Binstead Road.

You pass Westfield Park House, with the stag sculpture on top of the gateway, which was built in 1808 by the then Earl Spencer. It was converted into a hotel in 1936 and included gas-operated boilers to provide guests with instant hot water. As to be expected, it has now been converted into flats.

Along the way, Spencer Road loses its pavements and turns into a private road. There is still right-of-way for walkers so continue. When you reach the junction with Binstead Road, on your right are signposts for the '*Coastal Path*' between two driveways.

B Take this path, which is sheltered so is ideal for hot days, crossing over a small bridge, until you reach Holy Cross Binstead Church (*above*). The path curves to the left here, then to the right, and stay on Church Road until you see the signs for the '*Coastal Path*' on the right. Take this and, as you approach Kingnoth Lodge, the path breaks to the left of it. When the path joins the main track, bear right heading to Quarr Abbey until you reach the remains of the old Abbey, the 18th Century cottage (*below*), and the lodge building.

The original Abbey was founded in 1132 but 400 years later, when Henry VIII declared himself head of the English Church in 1534, the monasteries were stripped and - in most cases - torn down. The new brick abbey (*opposite top*) was constructed in 1912.

C If you want to cut three-quarters-of-a-mile from your walk, take the path heading alongside the field opposite Quarr Abbey Lodge on your left, but I do recommend continuing on the short distance to the 'new' Quarr Abbey itself. If you head to the Abbey, the path on your left opposite the lodge is where you come back to in a bit to continue the loop.

Abbey Visit: You will reach an information board on your right, with a car park on your left and a bench just ahead, this is the entry to the Abbey grounds. Take the gravel path on the right and follow it until you reach the entrance to the chapel, with the shop, visitor centre, art gallery, and café on your left. There are toilets and picnic benches here, and around to the left of the buildings are the pigs. If you neglected to bring any carrots or scraps with you, the shop sells pig food (£1.20 a bag) and if you shake the bag as you approach the pens they will come running.

When you have finished at the Abbey, head back the way you came until you reach Quarr Abbey Lodge again and take the path opposite (now on your right).

Follow the track away from the lodge as it goes past the old abbey walls and then into woodland. At the end, just through the gate, you need to cross the A3054 and pick up the track on the other side of the road. The fields you pass through are great for seeing birds-of-prey on summer days, so don't forget to look up.

Stick to the right-edge of the field border until you get to a gate at the end that takes you through another woodland section, passing two large ponds, and then reaches another gate leading into a field.

The path continues diagonally to your left across the field, but there can be cows in this field so feel free to stick to the left edge as you make your way to the gate across from you. As always with cows, please take care; if they think it is close to feeding time they will make their way to you, you just need to walk slowly away from them to the field edge.

Go through the gate at the edge of the field to the road, then go to your left (no pavement here), passing several bungalows until Newnham Road, where you turn left. A few houses along on your right is a narrow path heading down (marked by a bright red dog mess bin).

D When you reach a brown fence in front of you, head right, following the sign R40. At the junction the path you want jinks left then right, now following the R113. Stay on this through the woodlands (ignoring side paths) until you get to a crossroads. With the metal gate on your right, you want to head to the R38 (marked Play Lane) on your left. This takes you up a hill where it joins a tarmac road and carries on to your right, staying on the paved section past the school and sports fields.

Eventually you come to the main road. Take Partlands Avenue ahead of you, bearing left when it reaches Swanmore Road. Just after the second zebra crossing the road forks. Head down the left fork, West Street (heading for the church spire). You pass Ryde Cemetery and All Saints Church (*above*). Continue until you get to West Street, where you turn right and follow it past St. James' Church and the Ryde Theatre. Union Street on your left takes you back to the pier where you started.

Benches: For the first 3 miles

Picnic Areas: The beach, Quarr Abbey

Pubs: Start and end of walk

Public Toilets: Beach, Quarr Abbey

Cafe/Shop: Start/End and Quarr Abbey

Other Ways of Exploring

If you are looking for other ways to explore Portsmouth or find out more about her, you could try talking to Steve (*right*).

In the summer months you can find him in the mornings on the Hard, opposite the Ship Anson. He will give you a guided tour of the area, telling you about the people who lived there.

You can also book him in advance: portsmouthofthepast@btinternet.com.

In the summer, there is the Number 26 open-top bus which runs along the seafront. You can catch it at Clarence Pier and the ticket (£5 for adults and £3.50 for children) is open for the day so you can get on and off as much as you like.

Another way of exploring the harbour area is by boat, and www.portsmouth-boat-trips.co.uk do regular harbour tours where you pass the navy base, the commercial port, and they tell you the history of the area you are looking at as well. It costs £12 for adults and £7.50 for children (though it is included in the Ultimate Explorer ticket for Portsmouth Historic Dockyard). They depart from Gunwharf and the Historic Dockyard.

Finally, if you want something a bit different, try taking a tour of the harbour on the landing craft F8 (*above*). This runs from Boathouse 4 in the Historic Dockyard, check out their website for details of when they are running:

www.boathouse4.org/boat-charters/1127

World War One Remembrance Centre

A very important and often overlooked museum in Portsmouth is the World War One Remembrance Centre at Bastion #6, in the Hilsea Lines (see Page **41** to access it from the Hilsea Lines Walk). There is parking there if you want to drive directly to it, and is accessible from the Airport Service Road, postcode PO3 5PJ.

The museum is run by volunteers and relies on public donations, and you will need at least an hour to visit. Though small, the stories the guides tell to take you through the war are informative and often moving.

They don't just talk about acts of heroism rewarded with medals, they tell you about the everyday lives of the soldiers in the trenches, how Winnie the Pooh came to be written, and what the general populace back home were doing to cope with life when the world was at war. If you have been working on your family tree, and have discovered a WW1 connection, then the folks here can help you.

They run an education programme for schools, and the founder organises trips to the battlefields of the Somme and Ypres.

If you are a researcher, they have a library available for use, and are in the process of expanding their offering with a theatre area. As the Great War drops further into the past, it is important for everyone to understand the sacrifices given by all those, whether fighting or at home, in the attempt to bring peace to the world.

They also hold a ceremony on Remembrance Sunday to mark the fallen.

As it is run by volunteers, please check their Facebook page *WW1 Remembrance Centre* for opening hours when planning your visit, and if you have time on your hands, they always need volunteers to help out.

Appendix A – Walking Logs

Walk	Date	With	Notes
P1			
P2			
P3			
P4			
P5			
P6			
P7			
P8			
P9			
P10			
N1			
N2			
N3			
N4			
N5			
N6			
N6a			
E1			
E2			
E3			
E4			
E5			
G1			
G2			
G3			
G4			
W1			
W2			
W3			
W4			
W5			
S1			

Walk	Date	With	Notes
P1			
P2			
P3			
P4			
P5			
P6			
P7			
P8			
P9			
P10			
N1			
N2			
N3			
N4			
N5			
N6			
N6a			
E1			
E2			
E3			
E4			
E5			
G1			
G2			
G3			
G4			
W1			
W2			
W3			
W4			
W5			
S1			

3rd Century AD – Portus Adurni constructed by the Romans (now known as Portchester Castle).

1042 – The first recorded reference to Wymering Manor, recognised as the oldest building in Portsmouth, which is likely built on the remains of a Roman site.

1086 – Buckland, Copnor, Fratton, Wymering, Portchester, Fareham, Rowner, and Alverstoke, mentioned in the Domesday Book.

c1180 – Jean de Gisors owns land in what is now the Old Portsmouth area.

1188 – The medieval church that later formed the core of Portsmouth Cathedral was dedicated.

1194 – King Richard I grants Portsmouth a Royal Charter, allowing for an annual fair of 15 days, Thursday markets, and a local court.

1200's – Population of Portsmouth (just Portsea Island at this point) around 1,200 (total population of England under 3 million).

1212 – King John orders the existing dockyard at Portsmouth to be protected with a wall, making it a Royal dockyard.

1348 – The Black Death reaches Portsmouth (one of many outbreaks), after entering the country through ships arriving at Weymouth. It is estimated one-third of the population of England died in this outbreak.

1369 – The French raided and burnt parts of Portsmouth, which they would also repeat in 1377 and 1380.

1380 – The fortification of Portsmouth takes on a new urgency after another French raid, and wooden walls are constructed to help fortify key areas.

1418 – Construction, in wood, begins of the Round Tower.

1422 – A chain across the harbour was installed, so it could be raised from the seabed forming a tight barricade across the harbour mouth if Portsmouth was under threat.

9th January 1450 – The Bishop of Chichester, Adam Moleyns, was lynched on the beach near the Domus Dei, with one theory being for failing to pay soldiers wages.

1490 – The Round Tower is rebuilt in stone.

1494 – Construction starts on the Square Tower (stone).

1495 – The first recorded dry dock starts being built in Portsmouth.

1544 – Southsea Castle built on the orders of Henry VIII.

19th July 1545 – King Henry VIII, from Southsea Castle, watches the *Mary Rose* sink in the Solent.

1600 – Despite multiple outbreaks of plague, the population of Portsmouth (Portsea Island) is around 2,500 (total population of England estimated at around 4 million).

1623 – Prince Charles, later to become King Charles I, departs from Portsmouth to Spain to arrange a suitable marriage for himself.

5th October 1623 – The Prince returns from Spain (accompanied by George Villiers, the Duke of Buckingham), and he was greeted with '*the greatest joy possible*' by the citizens of Portsmouth.

23rd August 1628 – George Villiers, the Duke of Buckinghamshire, is assassinated by John Felton, an army officer passed over for promotion by Villiers.

1635 – Portsmouth presented with a gilded lead bust of Charles I to show his gratitude and affection for Portsmouth. The bust was mounted in the north-facing wall of the Square Tower, though was thought to be destroyed during the English Civil War. After the monarchy was restored, a replacement bust was put in place around 1660, which is now in the Portsmouth City Museum. The one in the wall of the square tower is a fibreglass copy.

12th August 1642 – The Siege of Portsmouth, by Parliamentarian forces in the English Civil War is under way, and on this day the bridge over Portsbridge Creek was captured, allowing troops to cross onto Portsea Island. The Royalist troops surrendered on September 4th, after Southsea Castle was captured.

14th May 1662 – Catherine of Braganza landed in Portsmouth prior to her marriage to Charles II. The first thing she asked for on arrival was a cup of tea!

21st May 1662 – Charles II married Catherine of Braganza at the Domus Dei (now known as the Royal Garrison Church) and the Governor's House - part of the dowry included Tangiers.

1673 - Louise de Kéroualle, a maid of honour to Charles II's sister, granted the title of Duchess of Portsmouth. By this time, she had been the King's mistress for two years and bore him a son, Charles Lennox, who became the first Duke of Richmond.

1732 – Portsmouth Grammar School founded.

15th December 1747 – Edward Legge elected as MP for Portsmouth – 87 days after he had died!

August 1759 – A large explosion at Southsea Castle killed 17. People were cooking in a room above the gunpowder stores, and sparks fell through the gaps in the floorboards...

10th March 1777 – James Aitken (aka John the Painter) executed by hanging at the dockyard gates for sabotaging Royal Naval dockyards.

29th August 1782 – *HMS Royal George* foundered whilst being careened (having the hull cleaned) off Spithead. Over 800 souls were lost (it is impossible to determine exact numbers as there were many families visiting the ship at the time), with many buried on the beach at Ryde.

23rd December 1787 – Captain Bligh, onboard *HMS Bounty*, leaves Portsmouth on an expedition to transport breadfruit.

14th September 1805 – Vice Admiral Lord Nelson leaves the George Hotel in Old Portsmouth to re-join *HMS Victory* and head towards his fate at the Battle of Trafalgar.

1811 – Population of Portsmouth around 41,000 (the population of Great Britain around 12 million people)

June 1814 – *The Meeting of the Allied Sovereigns*, when the heads of Europe and military leaders such as Wellington, gathered in Portsmouth to celebrate victory over Napoleon Bonaparte. He would only be in exile on Elba for another 9 months before escaping and starting the '*Hundred Days*', culminating in the Battle of Waterloo.

1823 – The Portsmouth and Arundel canal was completed, though the Portsea section was abandoned by 1830.

29th November 1841 – Gosport gets its railway station.

20th May 1845 – The last duel on English soil between two Englishmen took place at Browndown, Gosport.

14th June 1847 – Portsmouth gets its first railway station. A lot of the delay was down to the Army as they did not want a hole punctured through the Hilsea Line defences to accommodate the railway.

1849 – The last outbreak of Cholera strikes Portsmouth, killing over 800 citizens.

1860 – Construction of Palmerston's Follies begins to protect Portsmouth, the Isle of Wight, and the Solent. Four forts in the Solent were built, existing Portsmouth fortifications improved, six forts from Gosport to Fareham constructed, and Forts Wallington, Southwick, Purbrook, Nelson, and Widley built.

1861 – Population of Portsmouth around 94,800.

1877 – The *Portsmouth Evening News* is founded.

26th July 1879 – South Parade Pier opens.

June 1882 – Arthur Conan Doyle arrives in Portsmouth, eventually opening a GP surgery on Elm Grove.

1880 to 1883 – H.G. Wells was an apprentice at Hyde's Drapery Emporium, Southsea, which he described as "*the most unhappy, hopeless period of my life*".

1883 – Portsmouth's first public library opened - compare that to Manchester which was in 1852!

17th June 1886 – Canoe Lake opens.

1887 – '*A Study in Scarlet*', the first appearance of Sherlock Holmes by Arthur Conan Doyle, is published.

9th August 1890 – The current Portsmouth Guildhall officially opened (though it was heavily damaged in 1941 by incendiary bombs).

1891 – Population of Portsmouth around 161,500.

5th April 1898 – Portsmouth Football Club founded at 12 High Street, Old Portsmouth.

1904 – Construction started on a military hospital on Portsdown Hill, which would become Queen Alexandra Hospital.

2nd December 1906 – *HMS Dreadnought*, the first big-gun, steam turbine powered battleship, commissioned in Portsmouth, creating a new arms-race.

30th September 1907 – The Kings Theatre opened with a production of '*Charles I*'.

1911 – The first council houses in Portsmouth were built.

12th January 1922 – *HMS Victory* was taken into dry dock #2, never to return to sea.

1926 – Portsmouth granted city status.

1929 – The motto '*Heaven's Light Our Guide*' added to the Portsmouth coat-of-arms.

14th December 1930 – The first flight lands at the new Portsmouth Airport, though it does not officially open until 2nd July 1932.

1935 – Hilsea Lido opened.

29th April 1939 – Portsmouth FC beat Wolverhampton Wanderers 4-1 to win the FA Cup. They actually become the team to hold it the longest as WWII means the cup is not contested for again until 1946.

10th January 1941 – Portsmouth suffered her heaviest night of bombing, with 171 killed and over 3,000 left homeless.

10th March 1941 – A German bomb landed in the dry dock alongside *HMS Victory*, causing damage but avoiding a direct hit.

14th July 1950 – An explosion at Bedenham Ammunition Pier, north of Gosport, injured 19, destroyed 2 lighters and 9 barges, and damaged an area as far out as Cams Hall, Fareham.

22nd February 1956 – Portsmouth FC vs Newcastle United is the first ever League match played under floodlights.

1961 – Population of Portsmouth around 215,000.

21st December 1973 – The last official flight from Portsmouth Airport.

1976 – Portsmouth Central Library opened.

5th April 1982 – A task force leaves Portsmouth, led by *HMS Invincible*, to liberate the Falkland Islands.

1984 – Portsmouth Royal Dockyard downgraded and renamed Fleet Maintenance and Repair Organisation (FMRO).

29th July 1988 – Port Solent officially opened.

1992 – Portsmouth Polytechnic becomes the University of Portsmouth.

1996 – HMS Vernon closed, and redevelopment of the site started (opening as Gunwharf Quays in 2001).

2003 – Two JMW Turner paintings of Venice are actually identified as being paintings of Portsmouth (who knew the two were so easy to mix up!).

2005 – The Spinnaker Tower finally completed and opened (6 years late and unable to be called the Millennium Tower as first envisaged).

27th March 2010 – The last greyhound race took place at the stadium in Tipner, which opened in 1931.

Appendix C –Walking and Local History Resources

Portsmouth Ramblers: The Ramblers organise regular walks which should be easy for residents of Portsmouth to get to. The walks vary in length and difficulty, and they are a very sociable group: https://www.portsmouthramblers.org.uk/

Hampshire 40+ Walking Group: They do what they say, which is organising walks for the over 40's and, like Portsmouth Ramblers, the walks vary in length and location:

https://www.hampshirewalkers.org.uk/

Hampshire 20's & 30's Walking Group: Like the above group, but caters for those in their 20's and 30's: https://www.hantswalk.org.uk/

Victoria Park Tree Walk: More an exploration of the park than a full walk, but interesting nonetheless:

https://www.portsmouth.gov.uk/wp-content/uploads/2020/05/cul-victoriapark-treetrail-leaflet.pdf

Hayling Billy Trail: This walk follows the old railway track from Havant to the seafront on Hayling Island. This site covers walk **E3** with a huge amount of history and flora and fauna notes: http://haylingbillyheritage.org/

Property Trust Interactive Map: Explore the historic (and listed) buildings within Portsmouth Dockyard: http://www.pnbpropertytrust.org/propertymap.asp

Tide Times: Tide times and shipping movements (best for checking to see if the aircraft carriers or destroyers are in transit or due through the harbour):

https://www.royalnavy.mod.uk/qhm/portsmouth

Queen Elizabeth Country Park: Although outside of Portsmouth, QE Country Park is a 25-minute drive away (on a good day) and has plenty of walking routes, picnic areas, and more. If you desire hills to walk, this is the place for you:

https://www.hants.gov.uk/thingstodo/countryparks/qecp/explore

University of Portsmouth Historical Map Resources: Online maps of Portsmouth and the area from 1545 onwards: https://library.port.ac.uk/mapuseful.html

Memorials in Portsmouth: A comprehensive list of all the memorials and dedications in Portsmouth: www.memorialsinportsmouth.co.uk

Portsmouth History Association: Monthly talks on a wide variety of topics, not just Portsmouth-focussed:

https://www.history.org.uk/branches/resource/1775/portsmouth-branch-programme

Portsmouth and Gosport History Week: Usually the first week of August, a week-long celebration of local history with events, talks, and open access to historic buildings and sites:

https://portsmouthgosporthistory.com/

Heritage Open Days: Usually in September, historic buildings across the UK open to allow the public access. Gosport have a very good, and popular, programme for their events each year. It is worth subscribing to their notifications and booking early when sites become available: http://www.gosportheritage.co.uk/

The Liberty of Portsmouth and Portsea Island: This is an in-depth history of Portsmouth, written in 1908 but still worth a read:

https://www.british-history.ac.uk/vch/hants/vol3/pp172-192

Southsea Coastal Scheme: These are the group responsible for improving the coastal defences (against the sea, not the French!) in the area. They regularly post updates on progress, and on the historical finds they make, especially of the old fortifications and structures:

https://southseacoastalscheme.org.uk/

The Portsmouth Bomb Map: Portsmouth was heavily targeted by the Luftwaffe during World War II, and this interactive map gives you details of each of the bomb hits on the city:

https://pcc.dynamicmaps.co.uk/MapThatPublic/login.html?user=Hist

Portsmouth Literary Map: An interactive map of literary references to Portsmouth, whether it be authors or books or even scenes set in the city: https://litmap.nautoguide.com/#Home

Facebook Group: Memories of Bygone Portsmouth: A group that specialises in images and stories of Portsmouth from the past, a really good one that throws up snippets of interest.

Facebook Group: Portsmouth Past and Present: This group tends to have posts about more modern aspects of Portsmouth, but members are always quick to add comments about the history of an area or building.

Re-enactors: There are several re-enactment groups in the area, including Deeds of Arms (*above*), Historia Normannis, Weorod, Fort Cumberland Guard, and Legio Secvnda Avgvsta.

Bird Aware Solent

Bird Aware Solent work with local partners to monitor and mitigate effects on local wildlife caused by local housing requirements and tourism pressures. As well as their monitoring activities, they hold talks, walks, and more. They always need more volunteers and help to organise regular beach cleans:

https://birdaware.org/solent/

Hampshire & Isle of Wight Wildlife Trust

The HIWWT has been running for over 60 years and strive to protect and enhance the conditions for wildlife in our area. They are responsible for over 40 reserves, covering all sorts of environments. Their events include walks, talks, identification trips, training for group leaders, and more:

https://www.hiwwt.org.uk/

Identification Apps

For each of the below apps there are alternative options, these are the ones I use but you may find a different one suits your tastes better, so please look through the reviews for each.

PlantNet, for IOS and Android, can take one of your flower or leaf photos and attempt to match it to its database. Great for helping to learn the plants you see on your walks (if you have a data connection), or afterwards for logging your sightings.

iNaturalist, for IOS and Android, allows you to identify and record flora and fauna, and the information is added to a global database. This app is great if you want to add to the long-term studies of environmental changes.

iRecord Butterflies, for IOS and Android, allows you to identify and record your butterfly sightings, with the information being stored centrally to allow researchers to identify trends and at-risk species.

BirdNET, for IOS and Android, allows you to identify birds by recording their song and uploading in into the app.

Appendix E – The Long-Distance Trails

There are several existing long-distance trails that incorporate Portsmouth, some of which can be done in a day, some will take longer. Full details for all of these trails can be found on the Long-Distance Walkers Association web pages (www.ldwa.org.uk).

The Solent Way: This 60-mile route runs from Milford-On-Sea to Emsworth Harbour, and passes the Hard, along the seafront, and then up the Eastern side of Portsea Island:

https://www.hants.gov.uk/thingstodo/countryside/walking/solentway

The Pilgrim's Trail: This 29-mile walk follows the route pilgrims landing at Portsmouth would have taken to reach Winchester cathedral. It has a very good mix of downs (*above*) and forest along its course, and is well worth taking the time to do:

https://www.ldwa.org.uk/ldp/members/show_path.php?path_name=Pilgrims%27+Trail

The Shipwright's Way: This trail is 50 miles long and leads from Bentley Station (near Alton) down to Portsmouth Dockyard. It is an imagined route that a tree felled for shipbuilding would take, from the forest where it grew down to the shipyards to be used by the craftsmen of the Royal Navy. There are 20 specially commissioned sculptures along the way, and the trail is suitable for cyclists and walkers:

https://www.hants.gov.uk/thingstodo/countryside/walking/shipwrightsway

The Allan King Way: The Allan King Way, all 43 miles of it, goes from Portchester to Winchester, and was created in memory of one of the early members of the Hampshire Rambler's Association:

https://www.go4awalk.com/walks/national-trail-and-long-distance-path-walks/walks-on-the-allan-kings-way.php

The Coastal Path: The very long-distance path that covers England's coasts, in total just over 2.800 miles, so not one for the weekend! All of the Hampshire coastline is covered by this route:

https://www.nationaltrail.co.uk/en_GB/trails/england-coast-path/route-descriptions/

Let me, AJ Noon, take you through the historic dockyard in Portsmouth, telling you about the buildings, statues, and memorials of the publicly accessible areas of what was the Royal dockyard.

With over 800 years of history, this book brings you some of the stories that made Portsmouth and the Royal Navy in an easy-to-follow guide.

It also includes how to make the most of your visit, whether for ticketed attractions or walking around for free. Including accessibility information, food and drink, timings, tours, and the best bits for the kids.

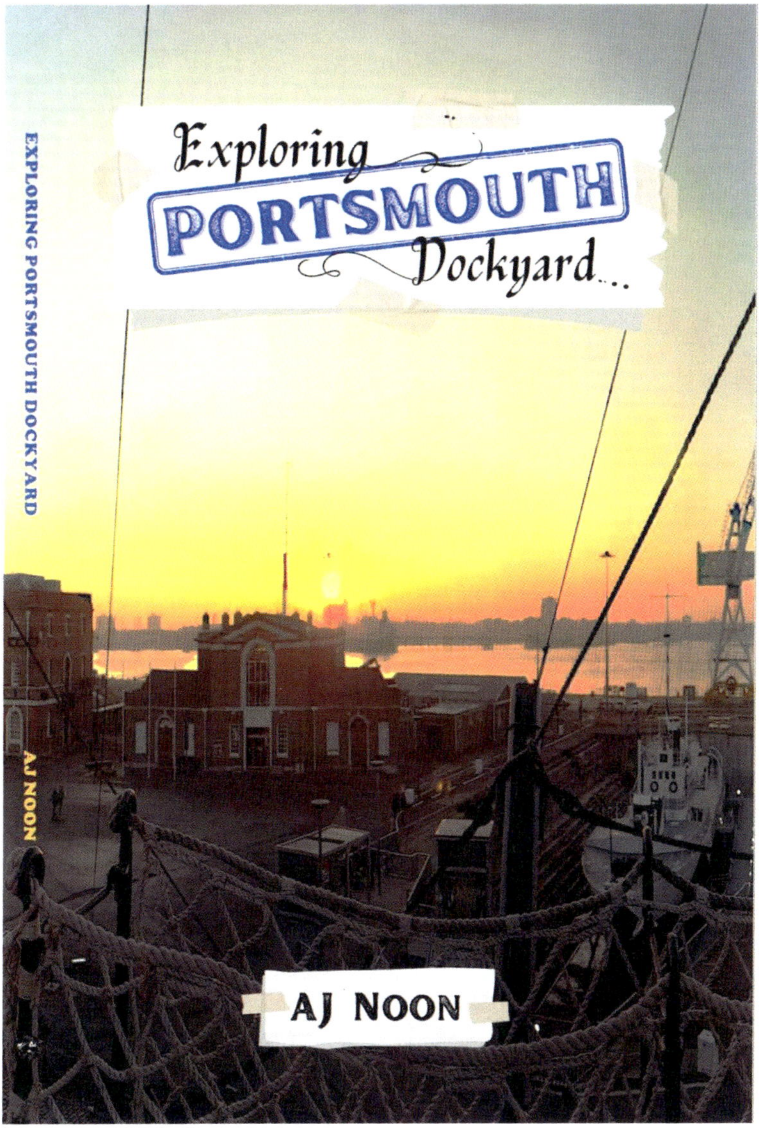

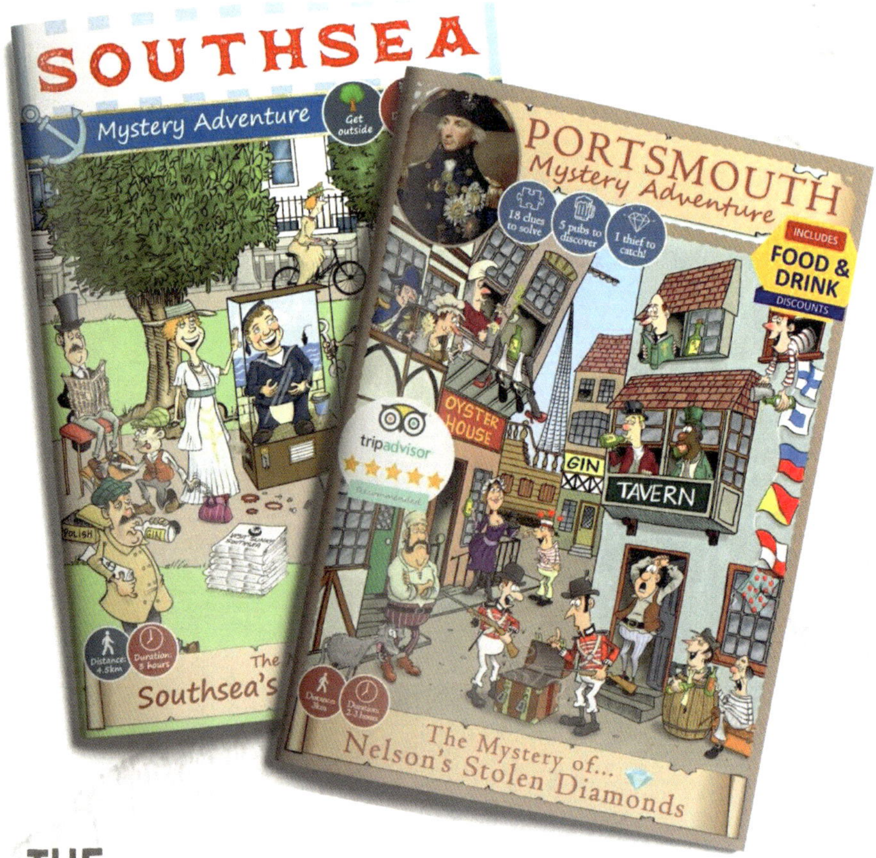
SOUTHSEA
Mystery Adventure
Get outside
Southsea's
PORTSMOUTH
Mystery Adventure
18 clues to solve
5 pubs to discover
1 thief to catch!
INCLUDES
FOOD & DRINK
DISCOUNTS
tripadvisor
OYSTER HOUSE
GIN
TAVERN
The Mystery of...
Nelson's Stolen Diamonds

Take a tour through the iconic ship that is arguably Portsmouth's most famous landmark, *HMS Victory*.

This book guides you deck-by-deck through the ship, bringing to life the wooden walls and the lives of the sailors who were on her.

Written by local author and guide AJ Noon, for every copy sold a donation is made to the National Museum of the Royal Navy, who look after the ship.